Ecodharma

ECODHARMA

*Buddhist
Teachings
for the
Ecological
Crisis*

DAVID R. LOY

Wisdom

Wisdom Publications
199 Elm Street
Somerville, MA 02144 USA
wisdomexperience.org
© 2018 David R. Loy
All rights reserved.

Library of Congress Cataloging-in-Publication Data
Names: Loy, David, 1947– author.
Title: Ecodharma: Buddhist teachings for the ecological crisis / David R.
    Loy.
Description: Somerville, MA: Wisdom Publications, 2019. | Includes index.
Identifiers: LCCN 2018022169 | ISBN 9781614293828 (pbk.: alk. paper)
Subjects: LCSH: Human ecology—Religious aspects—Buddhism. |
    Religious life—Buddhism.
Classification: LCC BQ4570.E23 L69 2019 | DDC 294.3/377—dc23
LC record available at https://lccn.loc.gov/2018022169

ISBN 978-1-61429-382-8   ebook ISBN 978-1-61429-398-9

24 23 22 21
5   4   3

Cover design by Phil Pascuzzo. Interior design by Graciela Galup.
Set in Whitman 11.5/15.25.

Printed on acid-free paper and meets the guidelines for permanence and durability of the Production Guidelines for Book Longevity of the Council on Library Resources.

Printed in the United States of America.

Please visit fscus.org.

For Joanna Macy,
Bhikkhu Bodhi,
Guhyapati,
and all other ecosattvas

There's good news and there's bad news. The bad news: civilization, as we know it, is about to end. Now the good news: civilization, as we know it, is about to end.

—SWAMI BEYONDANANDA (AKA STEVE BHAERMAN)

Contents

Author's Note

As readers of my other books may know, I'm fond of quotations. An insight precisely and succinctly expressed is something to savor. I encourage readers of this book to take the time to reflect on the quotations before every chapter.

Introduction

On a Precipice?

IT IS NO EXAGGERATION to say that today humanity faces its greatest challenge ever: in addition to burgeoning social crises, a self-inflicted ecological catastrophe threatens civilization as we know it and (according to some scientists) perhaps even our survival as a species. I hesitate to describe this as an *apocalypse* because that term is now associated with Christian millenarianism, but its original meaning certainly applies: literally, an *apocalypse* is "an uncovering," the disclosure of something hidden—in this case revealing the ominous consequences of what we have been doing to the earth and to ourselves.

Traditional Buddhist teachings help us wake up individually and realize our interdependence with others. Now we also need to consider how Buddhism can help us wake up and respond to this new predicament. And what does the eco-crisis imply about how we understand and practice Buddhism? Those are the themes this book explores.

The first chapter, "Is Climate Change the Problem?" offers an overview of our present situation. Although the overwhelming urgency of escalating climate change requires our unwavering attention and wholehearted efforts, we nonetheless need to realize that it is actually not the fundamental issue that confronts us today. That is because "global warming" is only part of a much larger environmental and social crisis that compels us to reflect on the values and direction of our now global civilization. It is necessary to emphasize this because many people assume that if we can just convert quickly enough to renewable sources of energy, our economy and society can continue to function indefinitely in much the same way. We need to realize that climate change is merely the proverbial tip of the iceberg, the most urgent symptom of a predicament that has more profound implications.

The chapter explores this by looking at what's happening with the oceans, agriculture, freshwater aquifers, persistent organic pollutants (POPs), nuclear accidents, radioactive waste, global population, and—of particular concern from a Buddhist perspective—the fact that we are already well into the planet's sixth great extinction event, in which a large percentage of the earth's plant and animal species are rapidly disappearing. This summary can offer only a snapshot: changes are happening so quickly that much of what I write is likely be outdated by the time this book is published. You can add your own "favorite" issue to this litany (the collapse of honeybee colonies, anyone?), but another dimension also needs to be emphasized: the "intersection" of these environmental issues with social justice concerns such as racism, ethnicity, gender, neocolonialism, and class. Recently it has become clearer that the ecological problems mentioned above, and the inequitable and hierarchical structures of most human societies, are not separate issues. The 2016 Standing Rock resistance movement in North Dakota, which brought together Native American "water protectors" with nonindigenous groups such as war veterans, was a watershed event in consolidating those movements. In the last few years American Buddhism has begun to address such concerns, including the lack of diversity within our own sanghas. This conversation is being led by an increasing number of teachers of color, who discuss the relevant social issues far better than I can do in this book—they include, for example, Mushim Ikeda, Zenju Earthlyn Manuel, Rod Owens, and angel Kyodo williams.

In response to ecological challenges, many Buddhist teachings can be cited, but this first chapter focuses on an issue that recurs in later chapters: the problem of means and ends. The extraordinary

irony is that we have become so obsessed with exploiting and abusing our actual treasure—a flourishing biosphere with healthy forests
and topsoil, lakes and oceans full of marine life, an unpolluted atmosphere—in order to maximize something that in itself has no value
whatsoever—namely, digital numbers in bank accounts. Because all
the world's economies are wholly owned subsidiaries of the earth's
biosphere, our preoccupation with ever-increasing production and
consumption is now disrupting the ecosystems of our planet.

Another important factor should not be overlooked: we abuse the
earth in the ways we do because our predominant worldview about
nature rationalizes that misuse. It is our collective (mis)understand-
ing of what the world is, and who we are, that encourages obsession
with economic growth and consumption. It is no coincidence that the
ecological crisis has developed when and where it has. Most of the
problems discussed in this chapter are connected to a questionable
mechanistic worldview that unreservedly exploits the natural world
because it attributes no inherent value to nature—or to humans, for
that matter, insofar as we too are viewed as nothing more than complex machines. This implies that the ecological crisis is something
more than a technological problem, or an economic problem, or a
political problem. It is also a collective spiritual crisis, and a potential
turning point in our history.

This brings us to the topic of chapter 2, "Is the Eco-Crisis Also a Buddhist Crisis?" The ecological and social challenges we face now go
far beyond the individual suffering that Buddhism has conventionally
been concerned with, so it is not surprising that Buddhist practitioners
and institutions have been slow to engage with those issues. On the
positive side, Buddhism clearly has the potential to do so. From the
beginning its basic teachings have emphasized impermanence and
insubstantiality, and this applies to itself. Buddhism is not just what
the Buddha said but what he began, and what he began soon spread
far beyond its birthplace by interacting with other cultures. Chan/Zen

Buddhism, for example, developed in China due to cross-fertilization between Mahayana Buddhism and indigenous Daoism. Today, however, the Asian Buddhist traditions face their greatest challenge ever, as they infiltrate a globalized, secular, hyper-technologized postmodern world that may be self-destructing.

On the negative side, some traditional Buddhist teachings discourage us from social and ecological engagement. If the spiritual goal is an individual salvation that involves not being reborn into this world of suffering, craving, and delusion, why should we be so concerned about what is happening here? In contrast to such an *otherworldly* orientation, however, many contemporary Buddhists doubt the existence of any transcendent reality and are skeptical of karma as an ethical law of cause-and-effect built into the way the universe functions. They understand the Buddhist path more psychologically, as a therapy that provides new perspectives on mental distress and new practices to promote *this-worldly* well-being. Otherworldly Buddhism (which aims to escape this world) and this-worldly Buddhism (which helps us harmonize with it better) seem like polar opposites, yet they usually share an indifference to the problems of this world. Neither is much concerned to help it become a better place.

There is another way to understand the essential teaching of Buddhism. Instead of trying to transcend this world, or fit into it better, we can awaken and experience the world, including ourselves, in a different way. This involves deconstructing and reconstructing the sense of self, or (more precisely) the relationship between oneself and one's world. Meditation deconstructs the self, because we "let go" of the habitual patterns of thinking, feeling, and acting that compose it. At the same time, our sense of self is reconstructed in daily life, by transforming the most important habitual patterns: our motivations, which affect not only how we relate to other people but how we actually perceive them and the world generally. In chapter 2 this alternative perspective is explored by unpacking an enigmatic aphorism of Chögyam Trungpa: "Enlightenment is like falling out of an airplane. The bad news is that there is no parachute. The good news is that there is no ground."

As we begin to wake up and realize that we are not separate from each other, nor from this wondrous earth, we realize that the ways we live together and relate to the earth need to be reconstructed too. That means not only social engagement as individuals helping other individuals, but finding ways to address the problematic economic and political structures that are deeply implicated in the eco-crisis and the social justice issues that confront us today. Ultimately the paths of personal transformation and social transformation are not really separate from each other. Engagement in the world is how our individual awakening blossoms, and how contemplative practices such as meditation ground our activism, transforming it into a spiritual path.

The Buddhist response to our ecological predicament is *ecodharma*, a new term for a new development of the Buddhist tradition. It combines ecological concerns (*eco*) with the teachings of Buddhism and related spiritual traditions (*dharma*). What that actually means, and what difference it makes in how we live and practice, is still unfolding, so this book emphasizes the three components or aspects that stand out for me: practicing in the natural world, exploring the eco-implications of Buddhist teachings, and embodying that understanding in the eco-activism that is needed today.

The importance of meditating in nature is often undervalued because its implications are overlooked. Chapter 3, "What Are We Overlooking?" reflects on why religious founders so often experience their spiritual transformation by leaving human society and going into the wilderness. Following his baptism, Jesus went into the desert where he fasted for forty days and nights alone. Muhammad's revelations occurred when he retreated into a cave, where he was visited by the archangel Gabriel. Perhaps the best example, however, is Gautama Buddha himself. After he left home, he lived in the forest, meditated in nature, and awakened under a tree next to a river. When Mara questioned his enlightenment, the Buddha didn't say anything but simply touched the earth as witness to his realization. Afterward he mostly lived and taught in the natural world—and he also died outdoors, beneath trees.

Today, in contrast, most of us meditate inside buildings with screened windows, which insulate us from insects, the hot sun, and chilling winds. There are many advantages to this, of course, but is something significant also lost? When we slow down and rediscover our primordial connection with nature, it becomes more evident that the world is not a collection of separate things but a confluence of natural processes that include us. Although we often view nature in a utilitarian way, the natural world is an interdependent community of living beings that invites us into a different kind of relationship.

The implication is that withdrawing into the natural world, especially by oneself, can disrupt our usual ways of seeing and open us up to an alternative. The world as we normally experience it is a psychological and social construct structured by the ways we use language to grasp objects. Names are not just labels; they identify things according to their functions, so we usually perceive our surroundings as a collection of utensils to be used to achieve our goals (such as satisfying desires). In doing this, however, we are constantly overlooking something important about the world, as William Blake knew:

> If the doors of perception were cleansed every thing would
> appear to man as it is, infinite.
> For man has closed himself up, till he sees all things thro'
> narrow chinks of his cavern.

Clinging to concepts, functions, and cravings is how we close ourselves up. In urban environments especially, almost everything we perceive is a utensil, including most people, whom we treat in a utilitarian way according to their function: the bus driver, shop clerk, and so on. In other words, we relate to almost everything and everyone as a *means* for obtaining or achieving something. Surrounded by so many other people busy doing the same thing, it is difficult to let go of this way of relating to the world, and experience it in a fresh way.

This has collective and institutional implications. Technologies extend our human faculties, including our abilities to instrumentalize the natural world. As the philosopher Michael Zimmerman writes,

"The same dualism that reduces things to objects for consciousness is at work in the humanism that reduces nature to raw material for mankind." This raises increasingly important questions about the concept of property, a social construct that should be reconsidered and reconstructed in light of our present situation. If an instrumentalist view of the natural world is at the core of our ecological predicament, perhaps the "liberation movement" most needed today is to appreciate that the planet and its magnificent web of life are much more than just a resource for the benefit of one species.

Many Buddhist teachings have obvious ecological applications. A life preoccupied with consumerism is incompatible with the Buddhist path. The five basic precepts begin with a pledge not to kill or harm life—not just humans but all sentient beings. The most fundamental principle of ecology—the interdependence of living beings and systems—is a subset of the most fundamental principle of Buddhist philosophy, that nothing has "self-existence" because everything is dependent on other things. Chapter 4, "Is It the Same Problem?" focuses on something that is less obvious: the profound parallels between our perennial personal predicament, according to traditional Buddhist teachings, and our ecological predicament today. I remarked above that the eco-crisis is as much a spiritual challenge as a technological and economic one; unpacking the similarities between our individual and collective predicaments helps to flesh out that claim.

Since our usual sense of self is a construct, it does not correspond to anything substantial, which is why it is inherently anxious and insecure: because there's nothing that could be secured. The self usually experiences this ungroundedness as a *lack*: the sense that there is something wrong with me, a basic discomfort often experienced on some level as *I'm not good enough*. Unfortunately, we often misunderstand our dis-ease and try to secure ourselves by identifying with things "outside" us that (we think) can provide the grounding we crave: money, material possessions, reputation, power, physical attractiveness, and so forth. Since none of them can actually ground or secure one's sense of self, no matter how much money (and so on) we may accumulate, it never seems to be enough.

The Buddhist solution to this predicament is not to get rid of the self, because there is no such thing to get rid of. As mentioned above, the *sense* of self needs to be deconstructed ("forgotten" in meditation) and reconstructed (replacing the "three poisons" of greed, ill will, and delusion with generosity, loving-kindness, and the wisdom that recognizes our interdependence). That is how we can see through the illusion of separation. If I am not something inside (behind the eyes or between the ears), then the outside is not outside.

Curiously, this Buddhist account of our individual predicament corresponds precisely to our ecological situation today. We not only have individual senses of self, we also have group selves, and "separate self = *dukkha* suffering" also holds true for our largest collective sense of self: the duality between us as a species, *Homo sapiens sapiens*, and the rest of the biosphere. Like the personal sense of self, human civilization is a construct that involves a collective sense of alienation from the natural world, which creates anxiety and confusion about what it means to be human. Our main response to that anxiety—the collective attempt to secure ourselves with economic growth and technological development ("progress")—is actually making things worse, because it reinforces our disconnection from the earth. Just as there is no self to get rid of, we cannot "return to nature" because we've never been apart from it, but we can realize our nonduality with it and begin to live in ways that accord with that realization.

But what collective transformation might correspond to the personal awakening that Buddhism has always promoted? "The Buddha attained individual awakening. Now we need a collective enlightenment to stop the course of destruction" (Thich Nhat Hanh). Isn't the idea of such a social transformation just a fantasy, given economic and political realities—or is it already happening, under our noses?

In his book *Blessed Unrest: How the Largest Movement in the World Came into Being, and Why No One Saw It Coming*, Paul Hawken documents what may be such a collective awakening. This "movement of movements" is a worldwide network of socially engaged organizations that has arisen in response to the global crises that threaten us today. It is both the largest ever—at least two million organizations, maybe many more—and the fastest growing. According to Hawken, "It's the first time in history that a movement of such scale and breadth has arisen from within every country, city, and culture in the world, with no leader, rulebook, or central headquarters. . . . It is vast and the issues broadly defined as social justice and the environment are not separate issues at all."

Hawken sees this movement as the "immune response" of humanity, arising as if spontaneously to protect us and the planet from the forces that are despoiling our world. The organizations that compose it are "social antibodies attaching themselves to the pathologies of power." As a Zen practitioner, Hawken sees Buddhism as a growing part of this movement: "Buddhism as an institution will become much more engaged in social issues, because I cannot see a future where conditions do not worsen for all of us. . . . *Dukkha*, suffering, has always been the crucible of transformation for those who practice." Buddhism is not about avoiding suffering but being transformed by it—which means there may be lots of transformation in our future.

Nonetheless, immune systems sometimes fail, and "this movement most certainly could fail as well." Diseases such as the human immunodeficiency virus (HIV) kill their host by destroying the body's immune system. That suggests less hopeful parallels, which brings us to the next chapter.

The title of chapter 5 is "What If It's Too Late?" James Lovelock, who first proposed the Gaia hypothesis, warned in 2009 that humanity could end up reduced to small groups living near the poles. He also believes that attempts to tackle climate change will not be able to solve the problem but merely buy us some time. Writing a few years later, Fred Guterl in *The Fate of the Species* and Clive Hamilton in *Requiem for a Species* are even more pessimistic, arguing that human extinction is a very real danger, because, as the Stanford biologist Paul Ehrlich bluntly puts it, "In pushing other species to extinction, humanity is busy sawing off the limb on which it perches." Are such predictions fantasies to scare us into action? They are not—but what *is* a fantasy is the widespread belief that the kind of industrial growth economy still promoted by the government of every (over)developed nation can continue indefinitely without wrecking the biosphere. The immediate threat to the climate is not only carbon emissions but "tipping points," such as the release of billions of tons of methane gas buried beneath permafrost that is now melting.

A few contemporary teachers have begun to address these existential concerns. Joanna Macy's "Work That Reconnects" emphasizes that our grief for what is happening to the earth is not the final collapse of our aspirations for it, but necessary for those who aspire to follow the path of spiritual engagement. Her 2012 book, *Active Hope,* integrates grief into a transformative spiral that starts with *coming from gratitude,* which enables us to *honor our pain for the world,* leading to *seeing with new eyes,* and only then *going forth* to engage in what she calls "The Great Turning." We must feel more deeply in order to be transformed more deeply.

Thich Nhat Hanh's response to the possibility of our own extinction encourages us to "touch eternity with our breath," for in that eternity there is no birth and no death. This is a basic Buddhist teaching that becomes even more important when considering not just our own individual mortality but that of our species. Many religions address fear of death by postulating a soul that does not perish with the body. The Buddhist denial of a soul or self (*anatta*) does not allow for that kind of immortality. Instead, you and I cannot die insofar as we were never born. As the Diamond Sutra states, when countless beings have been led to nirvana, actually no beings at all have been led to nirvana. Dogen, the great thirteenth-century Japanese Zen teacher, expresses this paradox best: "Just understand that birth and death is itself nirvana. There is nothing such as birth and death to be avoided; there is nothing such as nirvana to be sought. Only when you realize this are you free from birth and death."

Although such teachings traditionally focused on our individual situation, they have important implications for how we collectively relate to the ecological crisis. It is not only that you and I are unborn, for everything is unborn, including every species that has ever evolved, and all the ecosystems of the biosphere. From this perspective, nothing is lost when species including ourselves become extinct, and nothing is gained if our species survives and thrives.

And yet that perspective is not the only perspective. We are reminded of the Heart Sutra's pithy formulation: form is not other than emptiness, emptiness is not other than form. Yes, from the *shunyata* (emptiness) side, there is no better or worse, but that does not negate the fact that *emptiness is form*. What we call emptiness—the unlimited potential that can take any form, according to conditions—has taken form as this awesome, incredibly beautiful web of life, which includes us, and which should be cherished and protected. As the Heart Sutra also says, there is "no old age and death, and no end to old age and death." The spiritual path is living that paradox.

Chapter 6, "What Shall We Do?" considers what that actually means for how we respond to the ecological crisis. The short answer is that Buddhist teachings do not tell us *what* to do, but they tell us a lot about *how* to do it. Of course we would like more specific advice, but that's unrealistic, given the very different historical and cultural conditions within which Buddhism developed. The collective dukkha caused by an eco-crisis was never addressed because that particular issue never came up.

That does not mean "anything goes" from a Buddhist perspective. Our ends, no matter how noble, do not justify any means, because Buddhism challenges the distinction between them. Its main contributions to our social and ecological engagement are the guidelines for skillful action that the Theravada and Mahayana traditions offer. Although those guidelines have usually been understood in individual terms, the wisdom they embody is readily applicable to the more collective types of engaged practice and social transformation needed today. The five precepts of Theravada Buddhism (and Thich Nhat Hanh's engaged version of them) and the four "spiritual abodes" (*brahmaviharas*) are most relevant. The Mahayana tradition highlights the bodhisattva path, including the six "perfections" (generosity, discipline, patience, diligence, meditation, and wisdom). Perhaps the most important of all, Mahayana Buddhism emphasizes the practice of acting without attachment to the results. Taken together, these guidelines orient us as we undertake the *ecosattva path*.

Social engagement remains a challenge for many Buddhists, for the traditional teachings have focused on one's own peace of mind. On the other side, those committed to social action often experience fatigue, anger, depression, and burnout. The engaged bodhisattva/ecosattva path provides what each side needs, because it involves a double practice, inner (e.g., meditation) and outer (activism). Combining the two enables intense engagement with less frustration. Such activism also helps meditators avoid the trap of becoming preoccupied with their own mental condition and progress toward enlightenment. Insofar as a sense of separate self is the basic problem, compassionate commitment to the well-being of others, including other species, is an important part of the solution. Engagement with the world's problems is therefore not a distraction from our personal spiritual practice but can become an essential part of it.

The insight and equanimity cultivated by eco-bodhisattvas support what is most distinctive about Buddhist activism: acting without attachment to the results of action, something that is easily misunderstood to imply a casual attitude. Instead, our task is to do the very best we can, not knowing what the consequences will be—in fact, not knowing if our efforts will make any difference whatsoever. We don't know if what we do is important, but we do know that it's important for us to do it. Have we already passed ecological tipping points and civilization as we know it is doomed? We don't know, and that's okay. Of course we hope our efforts will bear fruit, but ultimately they are our openhearted gift to the earth.

It seems to me that, if contemporary Buddhists cannot or do not want to do this, then Buddhism is not what the world needs right now—but this book tries to show how much Buddhism can help us understand and respond to the greatest challenge that humanity has ever faced. And it also explores what that might mean for Buddhism today.

Everything is burning.

—The Buddha

We have entered the uncharted territory of a global emergency, where "business as usual" cannot continue. We must take the initiative to repair and protect this world, ensuring a safe climate future for all people and all species.

—Tenzin Gyatso, the Fourteenth Dalai Lama

My generation has done what no previous generation could do, because they lacked the technological power, and what no future generation will be able to do, because the planet will never again be so beautiful or abundant.

—Thomas Berry

If global changes caused by HIPPO (habitat destruction, invasive species, pollution, overpopulation, and overharvesting, in that order of importance) are not abated, half the species of plants and animals could be extinct or at least among the "living dead"—about to become extinct—by the end of the century. We are needlessly turning the gold we inherited from our forebears into straw, and for that we will be despised by our descendants.

—E. O. Wilson

The notion that science will save us is the chimera that allows the present generation to consume all the resources it wants, as if no generations will follow. It is the sedative that allows civilization to march so steadfastly toward environmental catastrophe. It forestalls the real solution, which will be in the hard, nontechnical work of changing human behavior.

—Kenneth Brower

Perhaps the way we respond to the crisis is part of the crisis.

—Bayo Akomolafe

The truth is green consumerism has made virtually no difference and shifts responsibility from the shoulders of the big polluters and governments that need to introduce the policies onto individuals. Individuals as citizens—that is, political actors—can be very effective because it is only through far-reaching mandated policy change that we will get anything like the response we need.

—CLIVE HAMILTON

What values ground our commitment to the idea that global warming will be solved if we can reduce atmospheric carbon dioxide to 350 ppm? Environmentalism is about deal-making in a moral abyss. The advantage in this is that because its concessions have taken the place of its values, it is able on occasion to declare victory and walk away from the wreck.

—CURTIS WHITE

We are a Star Wars civilization. We have Stone Age emotions. We have medieval institutions—most notably, the churches. And we have god-like technology. And this god-like technology is dragging us forward in ways that are totally unpredictable.

—E. O. WILSON

You cannot cut a deal with Mother Nature.

—MOHAMED NASHEED

Climate change is the greatest market failure the world has ever seen.

—NICHOLAS STERN

The economic and ecological meltdowns have the same cause: the unregulated free market and the ideas that greed is good and that the natural world is a resource for short-term private enrichment. The result has been deadly, toxic assets and a toxic atmosphere.

—GEORGE LAKOFF

The fundamental immaturity of the human species at this time in history is that our systems of governance and economics not only permit but actually encourage subsets of the whole (individuals and corporations) to benefit at the expense of the whole.

　　—MICHAEL DOWD

If nature were a bank, they would have already rescued it.

　　—EDUARDO GALEANO

An attitude toward life that seeks fulfillment in the single-minded pursuit of wealth—in short, materialism—does not fit into this world, because it contains within itself no limiting principle, while the environment in which it is placed is strictly limited.

　　—E. F. SCHUMACHER

Fundamentally, the task is to articulate not just an alternative set of policy proposals but an alternative worldview to rival the one at the heart of the ecological crisis—embedded in interdependence rather than hyper-individualism, reciprocity rather than dominance, and cooperation rather than hierarchy.

　　—NAOMI KLEIN

It is horrifying that we have to fight our own government to save the environment.

　　—ANSEL ADAMS

If people destroy something replaceable made by mankind, they are called vandals; if they destroy something irreplaceable made by God, they are called developers.

　　—JOSEPH WOOD KRUTCH

Someone needs to explain to me why wanting clean drinking water makes you an activist, and why proposing to destroy water with chemical warfare doesn't make a corporation a terrorist.

—Winona LaDuke

If a man walks in the woods for love of them half of each day, he is in danger of being regarded as a loafer. But if he spends his days as a speculator, shearing off those woods and making the earth bald before her time, he is deemed an industrious and enterprising citizen.

—Henry David Thoreau

Q: How many climate skeptics does it take to change a lightbulb?
A: None. It's too early to say if the lightbulb needs changing.
A: None. We only know how to screw the planet.

—Anonymous

Since the roots of our trouble are so largely religious, the remedy must also be religious, whether we call it that or not. We must rethink and refeel our nature and destiny.

—Lynn White Jr.

The more deeply I search for the roots of the global environmental crisis, the more I am convinced that it is an outer manifestation of an inner crisis that is, for lack of a better word, spiritual . . .

—Al Gore

The first step to reimagining a world gone terribly wrong would be to stop the annihilation of those who have a different imagination—an imagination that is outside of capitalism as well as communism. An imagination which has an altogether different understanding of what constitutes happiness and fulfillment.

—Arundhati Roy

What if global warming is a big hoax and we create a better world for nothing?

—question at climate change conference

1

Is Climate Change
the Problem?

LET'S BE CLEAR: climate change is the greatest challenge that humanity has ever faced. In fact, its implications are so momentous that the term *climate change* and its cozy cousin *global warming* become euphemisms for what is better described as a *climate emergency*. This book looks at the climate crisis through a Buddhist lens and also reflects on what that crisis means for how we understand and practice Buddhism today.

But is something even larger at stake than the climate emergency?

Despite persistent attempts by special interest groups to obfuscate the issue, the evidence provided by numerous scientific studies is conclusive and will not be debated here. Human civilization developed during what climate scientists call the Holocene era (the last 11,700 years or so), during which the climate has been generally stable and mild. Coincidence or not, agriculture began about 11,500 years ago, when crops such as wheat, barley, peas, and lentils began to be cultivated in the Levant. The Holocene is now ending, due primarily to increasing levels of carbon dioxide in the atmosphere (now well over 400 parts per million, in contrast to preindustrial levels of about 262 ppm) and in the oceans. This increase is mainly due to human activity: burning fossil fuels such as coal, oil, and methane gas. We are now living in the Anthropocene era, from *anthropo*, the Greek word for "human being." And, barring an unexpected natural catastrophe such as a meteor strike or the eruption of mega-volcanoes, it looks like the future of the biosphere for many thousands of years will depend on what humanity does (and does not do) in the next few decades—or is it the next few years?

Instead of repeating what most of us already know, let me just emphasize two fundamental points about the climate crisis. First, it is not an external problem that is happening to us but something we are doing to ourselves—though of course, some people and some societies are more responsible than others. About one-sixth of the world's population is so poor that they produce no significant amount of greenhouse gases. Tragically, it is such people in less-developed nations, mostly in Africa and South Asia, who have been suffering the most from climatic changes, whereas those living in the overdeveloped nations of North America and Europe have so far experienced relatively little disruption. We will return to the ethical implications of this difference, but my point here is simply that *Homo sapiens sapiens* cannot blame any other species, or natural disasters, for what is happening. Imagine how we would react if alien spaceships appeared and began pumping carbon dioxide into our atmosphere! Unfortunately, the root causes of our problem are not so easy to identify and attack. As Walt Kelly's Pogo said during the Vietnam War, "We have met the enemy and he is us."

My second point follows from the first: our collective response to the climate crisis, although not negligible, remains far from adequate. International conferences continue to be held and specific commitments have been agreed upon (and sometimes reneged upon), yet we are still not doing what needs to be done to reduce carbon emissions sufficiently. Given the extraordinary implications of the problem, we must ask: Why not?

Again, let me be clear: the overwhelming urgency of climate breakdown—no longer just a threat but something that has begun—requires our unwavering attention and wholehearted efforts. Nevertheless, we also need to realize that particular emergency is only part of a much bigger ecological crisis. *"Climate change" is not the fundamental issue that confronts us today.* I mentioned above that the climate crisis is the greatest challenge humanity has ever faced, that we are doing it to ourselves, and that our response so far has been far from adequate; all three of those points describe just as well the larger ecological challenge that is even more daunting.

It is necessary to emphasize this because many people assume that if we just convert to renewable sources of energy, our economy and society can continue to function indefinitely in much the same way that they have been doing. One problem with this way of thinking is that it takes up to a generation for the warming effects of new carbon emissions to register, which means that we can expect many more years of intensive climate disruption, with increasingly serious social and economic consequences that are very difficult to calculate. But the deeper problem is that the climate crisis is only the tip of an ecological iceberg that has more profound implications for the future of human civilization. From that broader perspective, we have so far been doing little more than rearranging deck chairs on the *Titanic*—a tired metaphor that nonetheless seems all too appropriate, given the increasing number of icebergs now calving in the Arctic and Antarctic.

Consider, for example, what is happening to the oceans. Of course, a lot of it has to do with increasing carbon emissions. Up to now, over 90 percent of the additional heat that has been generated by fossil fuel combustion has been absorbed by the oceans. Without that heat sink, average air temperatures around the globe would already have increased by a staggering 97 degrees Fahrenheit, by some calculations, and we would all be toast. The absorption of increasing amounts of carbon dioxide has also been acidifying ocean water (already more acid than any time in the last 800,000 years), disrupting the ability of mollusks and plankton at the bottom of the food chain to make their shells out of calcium carbonate. Most obviously, the potent combination of warming and acidifying water is bleaching coral reefs (which are home to a quarter of all marine species). According to the 2017 film *Chasing Coral*, the world has lost about half its coral reefs over the last thirty years, and almost all of the remaining coral is expected to die off during the next thirty years. Events in 2016 and 2017 severely damaged two-thirds of the Great Barrier Reef off the coast of Australia, and oceanographers are not hopeful of a recovery.

But there are other issues with the oceans. Global marine catches have been declining since 1996, and a study published in the peer-reviewed journal *Science* predicts that the oceans will be commercially fished out by 2048. According to a 2016 World Economic Forum report, by 2050 there will be more plastic in the oceans than fish, which points to another problem that cannot be attributed to carbon emissions. Less than half of the million plastic bottles purchased around the world every minute are recycled, according to a 2017 study reported in the *Guardian*, and annual consumption is predicted to exceed half a trillion by 2021. Since the 1950s approximately one billion tons of plastic have been discarded, and another 2015 study reported in *Science* calculated that eight million metric tons of it make their way into the oceans each year. The 2016 World Economic Forum report also estimates that there are over 165 million tons of plastic in the oceans today, much of it in an enormous vortex of microplastic debris in the Pacific Ocean, known as the Great Pacific Garbage Patch (and there is another in the North Atlantic). Unlike organic material, plastic does not biodegrade; it simply disintegrates into ever smaller pieces, which are often ingested by marine organisms, even in the deepest Pacific Ocean trenches—and by us. A 2017 scientific study found tiny plastic fibers in 83 percent of global tap water samples. The highest contamination rate was in the United States, with 94 percent.

There is also a worldwide problem with *hypertrophication*, when chemicals such as fertilizers and detergents run off into lakes and rivers, degrading the water quality and eventually leading to massive "dead zones" in bays and estuaries. Algal blooms, which are toxic to plants and animals including humans, are common and can cause fish kills and loss of species. A 2013 global assessment identified over six hundred such coastal zones around the world. One of the largest is at the mouth of the Mississippi River, which varies in size but is generally expanding; in the summer of 2017 it covered a record 8,776 square miles, according to the National Oceanic and Atmospheric Administration.

In sum, human activity is radically and rapidly altering the chemistry of the oceans, with ultimate consequences that are difficult to predict but unlikely to be beneficial either for marine life or for us.

And there are many other challenges.

Agriculture is the lifeblood of civilization as we know it, but in most places most people no longer live on family farms. The priority of industrial agriculture is maximum productivity at minimum cost, which requires intensive use of fertilizers, pesticides, and herbicides, such as Monsanto's notorious Roundup pesticide (glyphosate), now believed to be toxic to humans as well as honeybees and many other species. Yet there is a more basic problem, which the University of Sheffield's Grantham Centre for Sustainable Futures labels "catastrophic": a third of the world's arable land has been lost over the past forty years, at a time when the demand for food is soaring. "The continual ploughing of fields, combined with heavy use of fertilizers, has degraded soils across the world, the research found, with erosion occurring at a pace of up to 100 times greater than the rate of soil formation." Because of this deterioration, the UN's Food and Agriculture Organization predicts that the world on average has just sixty more years of growing crops, given present agricultural practices. To keep up with global food demand, the FAO estimates that about fifteen million acres of new farmland will be needed every year, but instead about thirty million acres are lost each year due to soil degradation. As if that were not enough, a 2014 study published in *Nature* found that increasing CO_2 in the atmosphere has led to a significant decline in the nutritional value of crops, especially protein, iron, and zinc.

As a Zen practitioner, I have often recited the bodhisattva vow "to save all living beings." And from a Buddhist perspective, perhaps no issue is of greater concern than the fact that we are now well into what scientists are calling the earth's sixth mass extinction event, when there is a widespread decline in biodiversity as many plant and animal species disappear. There is a wide range of views by biologists on how fast the extinction rate now is, but it is usually estimated as between one thousand and ten thousand times the "natural rate"— the rate at which extinctions would occur without human impact. According to a 2010 UN Environment Program report, one in four mammalian species, one in eight bird species, one in three amphibian species, and 70 percent of all the world's plant species are now endangered, mainly due to deforestation, agriculture, urbanization, and global warming. More recently, a 2016 World Wildlife Fund report concluded that populations of wild vertebrates fell 58 percent between 1970 and 2012, with losses on track to reach 67 percent by 2020. A study of German nature preserves found that insect abundance fell by 75 percent between 1989 and 2017. Most ominously, the eminent biologist E. O. Wilson of Harvard University has warned that by 2100 half of all plant and animal species on earth could become extinct or be so weakened that they will disappear soon after.

Enough already? Not quite. The list of human-induced problems is long; a few more follow, more briefly cited:

Lester Brown's research into groundwater highlights the fact that freshwater depletion is a worldwide problem, especially serious in Asia and the Americas. According to the FAO, global per capita freshwater availability is less than half of what it was in the early 1960s. Falling water tables and the over-pumping of aquifers threaten to end agriculture in arid regions such as the Middle East and the southwest United States.

In the last century many thousands of new chemicals have been created and marketed, but very few of them have been evaluated for their effects on humans or the environment. One category that has been researched is persistent organic pollutants (POPs), which do not naturally degrade but bioaccumulate, often with toxic effects. Some of them are endocrine disruptors causing developmental defects; others are known carcinogens or cause other chronic illnesses. And virtually all of us have at least traces of POPs in our bodies. So far, efforts to address this problem have focused on stopping the production and use of new POPs, since no one knows how to remove the POPs already in the environment. Recent research published in the journal *Nature Ecology and Evolution* has found "extraordinary" levels of POPs even in organisms that live in the deepest places in the oceans, the Mariana and Kermadec trenches.

Most of us are aware of the catastrophic 1986 nuclear explosion at Chernobyl in the former Soviet Union, which released enormous amounts of radioactivity into the atmosphere, and some of us remember the 1979 partial meltdown at Three Mile Island in Pennsylvania—but there have also been serious accidents at Kyshtym in the Soviet Union in 1957, at Windscale in the United Kingdom in 1957, at Chalk River in Canada in 1952, and at Tokaimura, Japan, in 1999. In March 2011 a magnitude-9 earthquake off the coast of Japan generated a tsunami that caused the meltdown of three nuclear reactors near the coastal city of Fukushima. Six years and many billions of dollars later, the situation remains out of control. The damaged reactors continue to generate high levels of radioactive waste (mostly contaminated water) and efforts to solve the problem have barely begun. As of late 2017, the plant's operator, Tepco, still had not been able to determine the exact location and condition of the melted fuel. Tepco expected the cleanup to take thirty to forty years, but Shaun Burnie, a Greenpeace nuclear specialist stationed in Japan, has said that such a decommissioning schedule was "never realistic or credible" because the challenge is "unprecedented and almost beyond comprehension."

In addition to such nuclear disasters, and the likelihood of more, almost 13,000 tons of highly dangerous waste (what Joanna Macy calls "poison fire") are produced by the world's four-hundred-plus active nuclear power plants each year. The United States has at least 108 radioactive sites designated as contaminated and unusable, some of them involving thousands of acres. The lifespan of some of the radioactive materials on these sites is very long: plutonium-239 has a half-life of 24,000 years, and, despite nuclear industry disinformation, no one really knows how to store this waste safely for the extremely long periods necessary.

And then there's overpopulation—an issue that no politician ever wants to talk about, because there are no votes to be gained by telling people that they should have fewer children. As of early 2018, world population is 7.6 billion, well over three times what it was at the end of the Second World War in 1945. The Global Footprint Network has calculated that the earth could sustainably provide only about two billion people with a European standard of living—and considerably fewer with an American lifestyle. This points to an essential concern, which we will return to: ecological stresses cannot be separated from social justice issues.

With only one exception that I'm aware of (about which, more below), all the world's major religions are pronatalist: they encourage people to go forth and multiply. That was understandable when our total impact was so much smaller. World population at the time of the Buddha was probably about 100 million people, about 1.3 percent of the current population, which continues to grow exponentially. We have solved the problem of perpetuating our species—so well, however, that our well-being, and perhaps our survival, are now threatened by our success. It is difficult to imagine how ecological sustainability could be achieved without a massive reduction, intentional or not, in our numbers. It is almost as difficult to imagine how that reduction can be achieved in a democratic and equitable manner.

The one religious exception to pronatalism is Buddhism. As far as I know, no traditional Buddhist teachings encourage families to produce many children. In some Buddhist societies the emphasis on celibate monasticism has had the opposite effect, tending to limit population growth.

One could go on and on, but this litany of ecological disaster is long enough. Perhaps the best summary of our situation is provided by James Gustav Speth, in the opening pages of his book *The Bridge at the Edge of the World: Capitalism, the Environment, and Crossing from Crisis to Sustainability*:

> Half the world's tropical and temperate forests are now gone.
> The rate of deforestation in the tropics continues at about an

acre a second, and has for decades. Half the planet's wetlands are gone. An estimated 90 percent of the large predator fish are gone, and 75 percent of marine fisheries are now over-fished or fished to capacity. Almost half of the corals are gone or are seriously threatened. Species are disappearing at rates about 1,000 times faster than normal. The planet has not seen such a spasm of extinction in sixty-five million years, since the dinosaurs disappeared. Desertification claims a Nebraska-sized area of productive capacity each year globally. Persistent toxic chemicals can now be found by the dozens in essentially each and every one of us.

[The United States] is losing 6,000 acres of open space every day, and 100,000 acres of wetlands every year. About a third of U.S. plant and animal species are threatened with extinction. Half of U.S. lakes and a third of its rivers still fail to meet the standards that by law should have been met by 1983. And we have done little to curb our wasteful energy habits or our huge population growth. . . . All we have to do to destroy the planet's climate and biota and leave a ruined world to our children and grandchildren is to keep doing exactly what we are doing today, with no growth in human population or the world economy. Just continue to generate greenhouse gases at current rates, just continue to impoverish ecosystems and release toxic chemicals at current rates, and the world in the latter part of this century won't be fit to live in. But human activities are not holding at current levels—they are accelerating, dramatically.

It's worth mentioning that Speth's book was published in 2008, which means that the problems he emphasizes *have* accelerated since he wrote about them. Our ecological situation continues to deteriorate, dramatically. Please note that what Speth emphasizes, and what I've written about overfishing, plastics, eutrophication, topsoil, species extinction, water depletion, POPs, nuclear waste, and overpopulation are all related to the climate crisis—because everything is, in one way or another—yet none of them can simply be reduced to it. Climate issues are receiving the most attention, and arguably are the most urgent, but they are nonetheless only part of a larger ecological crisis that will not be resolved even if we successfully convert to renewable sources of energy quickly enough to avoid lethal temperature increases and the other climate disruptions that will cause.

There is another dimension to the eco-crisis that needs to be emphasized. I have already alluded to it a few times: the "intersection" of environmental challenges with social justice concerns, especially racism, ethnicity, neocolonialism, gender, and class. The point of intersectionality—a more Buddhist term would be interrelationship, or interdependence—is that the ecological problems I've highlighted, and the inequitable and hierarchical structures of most human societies, are not separate issues. It is no coincidence, for example, that African Americans and other disadvantaged people in the United States are much more likely to live near waste dumps and other polluted sites. The lifestyles of the world's 500 million wealthiest people are responsible for almost half of all global carbon emissions, and some of that wealth is, of course, spent insulating themselves from the consequences of the climate crisis, which less fortunate people are already suffering from.

"Like the sinking of the *Titanic,* catastrophes are not democratic," said Henry I. Miller, a fellow at Stanford University's Hoover Institution. "A much higher fraction of passengers from the lower decks were lost. We'll see the same phenomenon with global warming." Justin Lin, chief economist at the World Bank, has estimated that 75–80 percent of the damage caused by global warming "will be suffered by developing countries, although they contribute only about one-third of greenhouse gases." Africa, for example, has been the source of less than 3 percent of global emissions since 1900, yet its 1.3 billion people (as of late 2017) are threatened by some of the biggest risks of water supply disruption, including drought and desertification.

"The inequity of this whole situation is really enormous if you look at who's responsible and who's suffering as a result," according to Rajendra Pachauri, former chairman of the UN's Intergovernmental

Panel on Climate Change (IPCC). Yet Michael Glantz, who studies climate hazards at the National Center for Atmospheric Research and has called for more research into adaptation to warming, is doubtful that much will be done to help poorer countries: "The third world has been on its own, and I think it pretty much will remain on its own."

Nonetheless, growing awareness of the relationship between the eco-crisis and social justice is opening up new possibilities. The Standing Rock movement in North Dakota in 2016, which brought together Native American "water protectors" from many different tribes with nonindigenous groups such as war veterans, was an important event in the consolidation of ecological and human rights issues. Rebecca Solnit writes:

> What's happening at Standing Rock feels like a new civil rights movement that takes place at the confluence of environmental and human rights and grows from the last 60 years of lived experience in popular power and changing the world. . . . Many involved in the climate movement see it as a human rights movement or a movement inseparable from human rights. Indigenous people have played a huge role, as the people in many of the places where extracting and transporting fossil fuel take place, as protectors of particular places and ecosystems from rivers to forests, from the Amazon to the Arctic, as people with a strong sense of the past and the future, of the deep time in which short-term profit turns into long-term damage, and of the rights of the collective over individual profit.

Of course, many other social issues should be added here: most obviously, the rapidly growing gap between a small, very wealthy global elite and everyone else, enabled by so-called democratic systems of governance deeply corrupted by a few powerful individuals and institutions. We should not be surprised that at the same time most of the world's "advanced" nations are experiencing skyrocketing usage of antidepressants and other drugs both legal and illegal, an unprecedented epidemic with consequences that are often fatal.

In short, even shifting one's focus from carbon emissions to the whole ecological crisis is incomplete and one-sided. There is something even greater at stake. One way to make this crucial point is to revisit the iceberg metaphor mentioned earlier. If climate breakdown is the very tip of the iceberg, the rest of the eco-crisis, including the social justice issues just mentioned, is below that tip—but still visible, above the waterline. So what is below the surface? Everything I have discussed so far can be understood as symptomatic of a more fundamental problem: the predicament of a now-global civilization that has lost its way and, despite its amazing technological achievements, seems to be self-destructing.

Thomas Berry has aptly described our condition: "We might summarize our present human situation by the simple statement: in the twentieth century the glory of the human has become the desolation of the earth, and now the desolation of the Earth is becoming the destiny of the human."

I locate this problem in the deeper, less visible portion of the iceberg, because we are normally unaware that our collective preoccupation with never-ending economic growth and consumerism—which have become in effect the most important goals of modernity, the *meaning* of our civilization—is incompatible with the finite ecosystems of the earth, of which we are a small part.

MEANS VERSUS ENDS

From a Buddhist perspective, many things can be said (and will be said later) about why this fixation on growth cannot provide the satisfaction we seek from it. But to understand better the relationship between the visible and the submerged parts of the iceberg—how the eco-crisis is a product of something even more problematic—let's briefly return to the oceans and look at one particularly revealing example of overfishing: bluefin tuna.

As you may know, Japanese love sashimi (raw fish), and their favorite is bluefin tuna. Unfortunately, overfishing has made bluefin tuna a highly endangered species (though the Japanese government has lobbied hard to avoid making that designation official). The "solution"? The Mitsubishi conglomerate, one of the world's largest corporate empires, came up with an ingenious response. It has cornered about 40 percent of the world market by obtaining as many bluefin tuna as it can, legally and illegally, despite its worldwide population plummeting toward extinction. Although this stock exceeds present demand, the tuna are imported and frozen at minus 60°C in Mitsubishi's freezers, for they will soon command astronomical prices if, as forecast, bluefin tuna become commercially extinct—due, of course to continued overfishing by tuna fleets trying to satisfy the insatiable demand, a large part of which is Mitsubishi's.

Ironically, when the 2011 tsunami struck Japan and destroyed the Fukushima Nuclear Plant, the electricity that supplied some of those freezers failed and thousands of tons of bluefin thawed and were lost. And exposure of illegal "harvesting" and smuggling has caused the reluctant Japanese authorities to impound some of the imports. But those have been only temporary setbacks.

From an ecological standpoint, Mitsubishi's response to the diminishing supply of bluefin tuna—in effect, aggravating the problem—is immoral, even obscene. From a narrow economic standpoint, however, it's quite logical, even clever, because the fewer bluefin tuna in the ocean, the more valuable Mitsubishi's frozen stock becomes. And it is the nature of economic competition that corporations like Mitsubishi are sometimes encouraged or "forced" to do things like that. If they don't do it, someone else probably will. In fact, Mitsubishi is not the only Japanese corporation freezing bluefin tuna, just the most conspicuous. That's how "the tragedy of the commons" tends to play out on a global scale.

Why do I emphasize this particular example? Because it points so clearly to the fundamental problem with the relationship between modern civilization and the natural world: the perversity of any economic system that devalues the biosphere (which humans are part of, of course) into a *means* for achieving something else. This problem is not unique to our capitalism, for the same problem existed in the Soviet Union and pre-capitalist China. Nor is it unique to modernity, for many civilizations throughout history (in contrast to some low-population First Nation societies) have exploited their environments to the extent that their technologies allowed. What *is* unique today is the combination of extraordinarily powerful technologies, unprecedented population growth, and an economic system that needs to keep expanding if it is to avoid collapse.

In our case, the perversity that traps us subordinates the natural world to the goal of profitability. Corporate capitalism has been amazingly creative and, for many of us, a source of considerable freedom and opportunity. Yet it has nonetheless become very problematic. Here and elsewhere in this book, I want to reflect particularly on the relationship between means and ends/goals. Ironically, what is especially interesting about the capitalist version of means-and-ends is that the *end* that is sought—profitability—is . . . actually only another *means*.

Profit, of course, means money. Because we use money every day, we think we understand it, but because its usage is integrated so seamlessly into the rest of our lives, we do not usually appreciate the fact that money in itself is worthless. We can't sleep under the paper bills in our wallets or eat the digital numbers in our bank accounts. At the same time, money is also the most valuable thing of all because it is our medium of exchange. It can be both worthless and the most valuable thing, at the same time, because money is a socially constructed (and legally enforced) *symbol*—arguably our most important one, for civilization as we know it could not function without it. It's like water, the "universal solvent" that enables one thing to transform into another. We can use money to acquire almost anything we may desire, which encourages a second function: as a storehouse of value, because we can accumulate (i.e., save) it.

There is something distasteful about loving money itself (rather than the specific things it can buy) because that is attachment to a symbol worthless in itself. The anthropologist Weston LaBarre called the "money complex" a psychosis that has been normalized, "an institutionalized dream that everyone is having at once." But since we unreflectively tend to equate the satisfaction of our desires with happiness, money psychologically, and perhaps inevitably, comes to represent the possibility of happiness. Money transforms into a "pure" means that swallows all ends: "abstract happiness" (as Schopenhauer put it)—therefore those unable to enjoy concrete happiness delight in accumulating it. Money becomes "frozen desire"—not desire for anything in particular, but a symbol for the satisfaction of desire in general. And what did the Buddha say about desire?

Ecologically, the problem is that our institutionalized fixation on profit and moneymaking now overshadows our appreciation of the natural world, which means that we have become obsessed with exploiting and misusing the actual treasure—a flourishing biosphere with healthy forests and topsoil, oceans full of marine life, and so on— in order to maximize numbers in bank accounts. *We end up sacrificing everything real for a symbol worthless in itself, exchanging what is most valuable for something that in itself has no value whatsoever.* And because of our collective preoccupation with that symbol, many of the things we want to buy with it may no longer be available in the future.

> When the last tree has been cut down, the last fish caught, the last river poisoned, only then will we realize that one cannot eat money. (Native American saying)

That points to why the whole eco-crisis is actually symptomatic of an even larger emergency, revealing the predicament of a civilization whose foremost obsession is incompatible with Buddhist values. The vicious logic I've just outlined implies that sooner or later our collective focus on profitability and endless growth—on ever-increasing production and consumption, which requires ever-more exploitation of "our natural resources"—must inevitably run up against the limits of the planet. "What the climate needs to avoid collapse is a contraction in humanity's use of resources; what our economic model demands to avoid collapse is unfettered expansion. Only one of these sets of rules can be changed, and it's not the laws of nature" (Naomi Klein). All the world's economies are wholly owned subsidiaries of the earth's biosphere, but we still don't get it.

Many Buddhist teachings are relevant here and will be discussed throughout this book. As a foretaste, there is the traditional emphasis on interdependence and nonduality. Both individually and collectively, we often pursue our own benefit at the cost of others' well-being in ways that the eco-crisis repudiates, because we're all in this together, or (better) because we're all part of each other. A planet carved up into over two hundred little gods (i.e., nations), each beholden to nothing greater than itself, yet bounded by the geographical limits and ambitions of the other gods around it, is always going to be problematic, and from an ecological perspective the nation-state system doesn't function very well today. When China burns coal, the air pollution produced doesn't remain only in Chinese skies, nor does radioactive water from the Fukushima nuclear disaster stay inside Japanese coastal waters.

The ecological crisis is rubbing our noses into the basic fact we keep trying to ignore: like it or not, in the most important sense we're all one.

The Loss of the Sacred

I mentioned earlier that our present relationship to the natural world—exploiting it as a means to other ends—is unique because of our especially powerful technologies, explosive population growth, and the need for our economic system to keep expanding. Another important factor must not be overlooked: we abuse the earth in the ways that we do because the predominant worldview about nature rationalizes that misuse. It is our understanding of what the world is, and who we are, that encourages obsession with economic growth and consumption, whatever the ecological price.

Of course we need to use the natural resources that the world provides in order to survive and thrive—that's what every other species does too, as well as it can. The ironic problem is that, even though we are completely dependent upon the natural world, humans feel separate from it. In believing ourselves to be *the* special species, we have objectified the world into an external environment that we just happen to be "in." In contrast, consider the perspective of most indigenous traditions. Many First Nation peoples express gratitude to the animals they catch for allowing themselves to be caught and eaten. According to a Salish legend, for example, salmon intentionally enter the human world to offer their bodies as food. "Salmon are themselves a proud race. They are happy to come ashore each year and give their rich flesh to feed the people, but they must be treated with respect." (Donna Joe, *Salmon Boy*) Invariably, a responsibility comes with that gift: not to take more than is needed. Today, however, our market economy knows no such restraints, because any idea of a reciprocal relationship with nonhuman beings is an outdated myth that we have outgrown. Or so we believe.

It is no coincidence that the ecological crisis has developed when and where it has, in a modern world that, when it comes to economic activity, is resolutely *secular*: this-worldly, irreligious, materialistic. Many people take such secularity for granted, assuming that, once superstitious beliefs have been removed, the modern secular view is an accurate account of what the world really is. But secularity is not simply the everyday world we actually dwell in. It is a historically conditioned understanding of where and what we are—a worldview, moreover, that becomes controversial when we look into its origins and implications.

The secular world that we now understand ourselves to be living in was originally one half of a duality, and it remains haunted by the loss of its other half. Modernity developed out of a split that developed between God's transcendence and a de-spiritualized material world. Until the modern era, God was believed to be the source of meaning and value, so when God eventually disappeared up into the clouds, we were left to cope as best we could in what was left: a desacralized mechanistic universe.

At the beginning of the Renaissance, Europeans still understood the earth and its creatures according to an organic and hierarchical paradigm. Everything, including human society, has its ordained place within a tiered cosmos created and sustained by God. "Natural philosophy," the old name for science, was a quest to understand the workings of God in the natural world. How does nature manifest God's mind and will? How do its beings embody God's "signature"? And, most important, what does this understanding of the world reveal about our role in it, the meaning of our lives? Notice that this spiritual perspective did not separate facts from values. The search to discover *what is* was not distinguished from our existential need to determine how we (as part of what is) should live. In God's cosmic plan they were nondual.

In the sixteenth and seventeenth centuries this medieval worldview collapsed, along with the institutions supporting it. This generated an enormous amount of anxiety. The rug was pulled out from beneath religion (the Reformation), government (widespread insurrections and revolution), war (gunpowder made warfare more aggressive), the economy (new business organizations, especially corporations, and the discovery of new lands), science (the collapse of Aristotelianism), and last but not least nature itself (an exceptional number of natural disasters—bad weather, poor harvests, famines, plagues—leading to riots, banditry, and so on).

The old order was dying, and no one knew what new order, if any, would replace it. The main characteristics of our modern world—including the nation-state, capitalism, and mechanistic science—developed and converged during the chaos of those centuries.

This crisis was initiated largely by the Protestant Reformation. Luther and Calvin eliminated the intricate web of mediation (by sacraments, priests, icons, holy days, monasticism, pilgrimages, and so forth) between God and this world—a network that had constituted, in effect, the sacred dimension of this world. For Protestant believers, mystery and miracle became de-emphasized in ways that opened the door for the materialist explanations of science and the materialistic concerns of capitalism. In *The Sacred Canopy*, Peter Berger describes this emerging worldview as one in which "reality is polarized between a radically transcendent divinity and a radically 'fallen' humanity that is devoid of sacred qualities. Between them lies an altogether 'natural' universe, God's creation to be sure, but in itself bereft of numinosity."

The result of this complex historical process (which I'm simplifying, of course) is that religion became, in an important sense, privatized. God came to be understood as dwelling far above the sordid affairs of this corrupted world but also deep inside the human heart. God was booted upstairs, even as the principle of a direct and personal relationship with God became sanctified. "Every man is his own priest," declared Luther. But where God all but ceased to dwell was in our political and economic institutions, and in the natural world. As the theologian Dan Maguire put it in *Ethics for a Small Planet*: "To project the experience of the sacred onto an immaterial God is to shortchange sacredness as a dimension of material life and turn it into an object of worship that is beyond our world and thus alien to life." And beyond the ecosystems of the earth.

Nevertheless, the early scientists most responsible for the new worldview—Copernicus, Galileo, Kepler, Newton—were also deeply religious and understood this world in relationship to a higher one. They all still believed in a Creator, although an increasingly distant one. They developed a new paradigm: God rules the universe not through a hierarchy of spiritual subordinates but with a rational system of "hidden laws." We use the same word for *laws* passed by a legislature and the *laws* of nature because the architects of the modern view believed that natural laws were also ordained, by God. Whereas the medieval worldview saw the influence of God filtering through agents (e.g., angels) of varying degrees of blessedness and power, the great Geometer was not to be identified with the fallen world he ruled impersonally from afar. As the astronomer Johannes Kepler wrote: "My aim is to show that the celestial machine is to be likened not to a divine organism but to a clockwork." And once God wound that clockwork up, God was not needed to keep it ticking.

Since God was the ultimate source of all goodness, this was also the origin of an increasingly sharp split between fact and value. As the

Deity gradually disappeared into the heavens, the material world left behind slowly but surely became devalued. This opened up exciting new possibilities. Those who comprehended God's hidden laws could use them to manipulate nature for their own purposes. But there was a downside. "The process of mechanizing the world picture removed the controls over environmental exploitation that were an inherent part of the organic view that nature was alive, sensitive, and responsive to human action" (Carolyn Merchant). The trajectory that would lead to our ecological crisis was set.

For the Protestant reformers secular life in this world was a preparation for our ultimate destiny: eternity with God in a better place. The evaporation of that sacred dimension—of God, the guarantor that life is meaningful and salvation possible—has left us with only the secular dimension. Modern consciousness became bereft of the spiritual orientation that the Reformation originally promoted.

With Darwin the transition to a secular ethic became complete. Darwin refuted the "argument from design," the last remaining proof for God's existence. Because evolution by natural selection doesn't need a God to direct it, an all-powerful Deity was no longer necessary to create the extraordinarily complex organisms, including us, that compose the web of life. In fact, the new secular world had no need for God at all.

That final Darwinian stroke left the modern West stranded, for better or worse, in a mechanistic and desacralized world, without any binding moral code to regulate how people relate to each other. The new secular universe, ruled by impersonal physical laws, is indifferent to us and our fate. Death is no longer the portal to another reality, just the end of this one. We may not as individuals believe that or feel personally oppressed by its implications, but secularization continues to remold our economic, political, and educational institutions. As this modern mindset spreads beyond the West, it increasingly determines the social environment within which people around the globe must live and act.

Although Darwin himself was troubled by the religious implications of his work, his theory was soon used to rationalize a new social ethic. Human life, too, is a struggle, in which only the fittest survive and thrive. This rationalized the most ruthless forms of economic and political competition, as recent history shows. As noted earlier, if Mitsubishi doesn't corner the (legal and illegal) market in bluefin tuna, some other corporation probably will.

Furthermore, if humans are mere accidents of genetic mutation and we have no special role to play in a meaningless mechanistic cosmos, what is there to do except enjoy our material possibilities as much as we can, as long as we can . . . if we can? This in turn leads to collective preoccupation with ever-increasing production and consumption, in competition with others seeking access to the same resources and opportunities.

The above understanding of where and what we are is part of the submerged iceberg of underlying causes that I mentioned earlier. We usually take it for granted as just the way the world is, rather than one viewpoint that recently has become questionable. Many premodern civilizations, with very different worldviews, have experienced their own ecological breakdowns, sometimes due to exhaustion of natural resources (see Jared Diamond's *Collapse* for some historical accounts). Today, however, it is clear that a mechanistic understanding of an objectified natural world, which we have no intimate relationship with and therefore no responsibility to or for, is an important part of the ecological crisis, and challenging that worldview must be part of the solution.

Buddhism originated in Asia and developed in very different cultural contexts, so its perspectives do not fit neatly into this history. Buddhist teachings do not support an Abrahamic-type Creator God, but neither do its traditional worldviews accord comfortably with the atheist or agnostic alternatives provided by secular modernity. The Buddhist approach that will be offered in the next chapter is much more compatible with alternative perspectives that question secular materialism without advocating return to the idea of a transcendent Mechanic.

According to the prevalent secular paradigm, biological evolution is the result of physical processes operating according to impersonal laws. It is a mechanistic model. But what if, instead of reducing biology to physics and viewing the cosmos as a machine, we try to understand the physical universe according to a biological model—that is, as *alive*? As Joseph Campbell observed, "If you want to change the world, you have to change the metaphor."

In fact, there is a fundamental problem with the mechanistic model. A machine presupposes a machine-*maker*: someone who designs and constructs it. A machine-like cosmos made sense as long as the universe was understood as having been created by God according to God's own plan and purposes. That was how the founders of modern science—Galileo, Kepler, Descartes, Newton, and others—understood the laws of nature. Without a Creator, however, a mechanical metaphor doesn't really make sense. So what other models are possible? Insofar as the universe constantly evolves new and more complex structures, is it better understood as an *organism*?

The different metaphors have very different implications. Machines can be disassembled into their components, cleaned, and after reassembly they work better than ever—but don't try that with an animal! That is because the various parts of a mechanism are lifeless in themselves but an organism is alive. And the components of an organism are better understood as *organs*.

This is more consistent with Indra's Net, a Mahayana metaphor that compares the cosmos to a multidimensional web with a jewel at each knot. Each of these jewels reflects all the others, and each of those reflections also reflects all the other reflections, ad infinitum. According to Francis Cook in *Hua-Yen Buddhism*, Indra's Net "symbolizes a cosmos in which there is an infinitely repeated interrelationship among all the members of the cosmos." Because the totality is a vast body of members each sustaining and defining all the others, "the cosmos is, in short, a self-creating, self-maintaining, and self-defining organism." In biological language, such a cosmos is *self-organizing*.

If the cosmos is a self-organizing organism, perhaps the earth too is something more than a place where we just happen to reside, more than a source of resources to be exploited as we like. Does that also mean that our species is something more than the accidental product of random genetic mutation? An organ is a collection of tissues forming a structural unit that has a specific function within the larger organism. Are human beings an organ within the Great Organism? If so, what is our function?

We shall return to these questions.

A Spiritual Crisis

This chapter has argued that, urgent though it is, the climate crisis is only part of a much larger challenge that includes overfishing, plastic pollution, hypertrophication, topsoil exhaustion, species extinction, freshwater depletion, hormone-disrupting POPs, nuclear waste, overpopulation, and (add your own "favorite" here . . .), among numerous other ecological and social problems that could be mentioned. Most if not all of these disorders are connected to a questionable mechanistic worldview that freely exploits the natural world because it attributes no inherent value to nature—or to us, for that matter, insofar as humans too are understood to be nothing more than complex machines, according to the predominant materialistic understanding.

This larger view implies that we have something more than a technological problem, or an economic problem, or a political problem, or a worldview problem. Earlier I suggested that modern civilization is self-destructing because it has lost its way. There is another way to characterize that: humanity is experiencing a collective *spiritual* crisis.

Traditional Buddhist teachings understand our fundamental problem in individual terms. My dukkha (suffering) is due to my own karma, craving, and ignorance, and therefore the path to resolve them is also individual. The idea of a civilizational crisis—of collective, institutionalized dukkha that must also be addressed collectively—is new to Buddhism but nonetheless unavoidable, given our precarious situation. The challenge that confronts us is spiritual because it goes to the very heart of how we understand the world, including our place and role in this world. Is the eco-crisis the earth's way of telling us to "wake up or suffer the consequences"?

If so, we cannot expect that what we seek can be provided by a technological solution, or an economic solution, or a political solution, or a new scientific worldview, either by themselves or in concert with the others. Whatever the way forward may be, it will need to incorporate those contributions, to be sure, but something more is called for.

This is where Buddhism has something important to offer. Yet the ecological crisis is also a crisis for how we understand and practice Buddhism, which today needs to clarify its essential message if it is to fulfill its liberative potential in our modern, secular, endangered world.

Does Buddhism itself need to wake up?

All of us are apprenticed to the same teacher that the religious institutions originally worked with: reality.

—GARY SNYDER

Perhaps in a very real sense, a great institution is the tomb of the founder. . . . Most organizations appear as bodies founded for the painless extinction of ideas of the founders.

—ALBERT GUERARD

Earth has no escape from heaven. Flee it up or flee it down, heaven invades it, energizes it, makes it sacred.

—MEISTER ECKHART

One does not become fully human painlessly.

—ROLLO MAY

If you bring forth what is within you, what you bring forth will save you. If you do not bring forth what is within you, what you do not bring forth will destroy you.

—JESUS IN THE GOSPEL OF THOMAS

One who truly renounces actually merges in the world and expands his love to embrace the whole world . . . you will feel that the whole world is your home.

—RAMANA MAHARSHI

Wisdom says "I am nothing." Love says "I am everything." Between these two my life flows.

—NISARGADATTA

When you know who you are, then you can be of some use.

—LINJI

2

Is the Eco-Crisis
Also a Buddhist Crisis?

THE PREVIOUS CHAPTER talked about an iceberg—not a real iceberg, such as those calving in record numbers off Antarctica, but a metaphorical one, to take advantage of the well-known fact that only a fraction of an iceberg is visible above the waterline. This analogy was used to explain our situation today. At the very top, the tip of what we can see, is the climate emergency. Below that but still above sea level is the rest of the ecological crisis, intertwined with social justice issues. Submerged, and usually unnoticed, is the largest part, the fundamental problem: a now-global civilization that has lost its way and seems to be self-destructing.

This chapter discusses another iceberg: Buddhism itself. Given the ways that the Buddha's teachings and the movement he founded have evolved historically and geographically, however, it might be better to speak of "Buddhist traditions" or even "Buddhisms." The multiplicity of Buddhist perspectives is very much to the point here, because they imply different ways of responding to the ecological challenge. It is important to remember, too, that all traditional Buddhist sutras and commentaries are premodern. Some doctrines are more compatible with what we now understand (or believe) about the nature of the world; by no coincidence, these are the ones that seem to be most pertinent to our situation today. Given the diversity of teachings, it's not possible to avoid emphasizing some more than others.

But this does not mean that Buddhist perspectives are to be subordinated to modern (or postmodern) viewpoints. The dialogue becomes most valuable when each side interrogates what the other takes for granted—which the ecological crisis prompts us to do, and which this chapter attempts to do.

At the very tip of the Buddhist iceberg, corresponding to the climate crisis, let's put this new development called *ecodharma*, which explores those aspects of the teachings that can best help us understand and address the eco-crisis. Making this relatively new term so prominent already suggests a question. The environmental crisis is not a recent development and has been front-page news for over half a century. Rachel Carson's *Silent Spring*, published in 1962, documented the detrimental effects of pesticides and inspired the creation of the U.S. Environmental Protection Agency in 1970. James Hansen testified to Congress in 1986 about the urgency of the climate crisis, and that issue became much more prominent with the Earth Summit in Rio de Janeiro in 1992. In my experience, however, most Buddhist practitioners and Buddhist groups did not become very concerned about the eco-crisis until after 2010, at least not in the United States, and I doubt that it was much different with Buddhist groups in other developed countries.

In 2009 Wisdom Publications released an anthology titled *A Buddhist Response to the Climate Emergency*, coedited by John Stanley, Gyurme Dorje, and myself. Like most compilations, it was a mixed bag, but it included fine contributions by the Dalai Lama, Thich Nhat Hanh, the Karmapa and several other prominent Tibetan teachers—Bhikkhu Bodhi, Joanna Macy, Robert Aitken, Matthieu Ricard, and Joseph Goldstein, among others. Nevertheless, and to our surprise, it aroused almost no interest in the Buddhist community. When I ask people at my talks and workshops whether they've seen it or even heard of it, almost all shake their heads. Around the same time as the book was published, I began offering workshops and meditation retreats focused on ecodharma and Buddhist social engagement. Many of them were canceled (or should have been canceled) because so few people signed up. I wondered if that revealed more about me than the issues themselves, but that's not been only my experience. In the last few years, interest in ecodharma has increased dramatically among U.S. Dharma teachers, and most of them report the same reaction: when the announced topic for a forthcoming dharma talk is Buddhism and the environment, the attendance is smaller than usual. *Why?*

Perhaps the foremost Buddhist organization in the United States explicitly focusing on ecological problems is One Earth Sangha, founded by Kristin Barker and Lou Leonard in 2013. Most recently, the Rocky Mountain Ecodharma Retreat Center opened in 2017 near Boulder, Colorado. Both are doing important work—and both continue to struggle financially. Evidently supporting them is a low priority for American Buddhists.

Just as climate change is only part of a much larger ecological crisis, so ecodharma is a small part of socially engaged Buddhism, and indifference or resistance to ecodharma is part of a larger problem with socially engaged Buddhism in the United States. In the wake of the Great Recession of 2008 the two largest engaged Buddhist organizations, the Buddhist Peace Fellowship and the Zen Peacemakers, almost collapsed due to severely reduced financial support, and since then they have struggled on—often quite effectively, I'm pleased to add—in much reduced circumstances. Noticeably, however, some other Buddhist institutions are thriving financially. In the last few years, for example, Spirit Rock in Northern California successfully fundraised for a multimillion-dollar expansion program. Noticing this difference is by no means a criticism of that accomplishment, yet the contrast in public support is striking. Serious money is available for some high-profile meditation centers, where individuals can go on retreat, but apparently not for organizations that seek to promote the social and ecological implications of Buddhist teachings.

This doesn't mean that socially engaged Buddhism has failed. In some ways it may be a victim of its own success, in that some forms of *service*—prison work, hospice care, homeless kitchens, and so on—

are now widely acknowledged as a part, sometimes even an important part, of the Buddhist path. Note that this is usually individuals helping other individuals. My perception is that over the last generation Buddhists have become much better at pulling drowning people out of the river, but—and here's the problem—we aren't much better at asking why there are so many more people drowning. Prison Dharma groups help individual inmates who are sometimes very eager to learn about Buddhism, but such groups do nothing to address the structural problems with our criminal justice system, including racial disparities and overcrowding. In 2014 the number of homeless children in the United States attending school set a new record: about 1.36 million, almost double the number in 2006–2007. Why does by far the wealthiest country in human history have so many homeless schoolchildren and by far the world's largest prison population?

Buddhists are better at pulling individual people out of the river because that is what Buddhism traditionally emphasizes. We are taught to let go of our preconceptions in order to experience more immediately what's happening right here and now; when we encounter a homeless person who is suffering, for example, we should respond compassionately. But how do we respond compassionately to a social system that is creating more homeless people? Analyzing institutions and evaluating policies involves conceptualizing in ways that traditional Buddhist practices do not encourage.

A similar disparity applies to the ways that Buddhists have responded to the climate crisis and other ecological issues. My guess is that most of the people who read this book have so far been little impacted personally by global warming, except perhaps for slightly larger air-conditioning bills. We have not personally observed disappearing ice in the Arctic or melting permafrost in the tundra, nor have we become climate refugees because rising sea levels are flooding our homes. For the most part, the consequences are being felt elsewhere, by others less fortunate. Traditional Buddhism focuses on individual dukkha due to one's individual karma and craving. Collective karma and institutional causes of dukkha are more difficult to address, both doctrinally and politically.

I'm reminded of a well-known comment by the Brazilian archbishop Dom Helder Camara: "When I give food to the poor, they call me a saint. When I ask why the poor have no food, they call me a communist." Is there a Buddhist version? Perhaps this: "When Buddhists help homeless people and prison inmates, they are called bodhisattvas. But when Buddhists ask *why* there are so many more homeless, so many people of color stuck in prison, other Buddhists call them leftists or radicals—saying that such social action has nothing to do with Buddhism."

Perhaps the individual *service* equivalent that applies to the climate emergency is personal lifestyle changes, such as buying hybrid or electric cars, installing solar panels, vegetarianism, eating locally grown food, and so on. Such "green consumption" is important, of course, yet individual transformation by itself will never be enough.

As Bill McKibben writes,

> We simply can't move fast enough, one by one, to make any real difference in how the atmosphere comes out. Here's the math, obviously imprecise: maybe 10 percent of the population cares enough to make strenuous efforts to change— maybe 15 percent. If they all do all they can, in their homes and offices and so forth, then, well . . . nothing much shifts. The trajectory of our climate horror stays about the same.
>
> But if 10 percent of people, once they've changed the light bulbs, work all-out to change the system? That's enough. That's more than enough.

Returning to the Buddhist iceberg, all types of social engagement, including ecodharma, form the tip at the top. Beneath them, but still above sea level, is something much bigger and still growing: the mindfulness movement, which has been incredibly successful over the last few years. Within the Buddhist world, however, it has also become increasingly controversial. Here I will not delve into that debate except to note that, although mindfulness practices can be very beneficial, they can also discourage critical reflection on the institutional causes of collective suffering, what might be called *social dukkha*. Bhikkhu Bodhi's warning about the appropriation of Buddhist teachings applies even more to the commodification of the mindfulness movement, insofar as that movement has divested itself of the ethical context that Buddhism traditionally provides: "absent a sharp social critique, Buddhist practices could easily be used to justify and stabilize the status quo, becoming a reinforcement of consumer capitalism." In other words, Buddhist mindfulness practices can be employed to normalize our obsession with ever-increasing production and consumption. In both cases the focus on personal transformation can turn our attention away from the importance of social transformation.

The contrast between the extraordinary impact of the mindfulness movement and the much smaller influence of socially engaged Buddhism is striking. Why has the one been so successful, while the other limps along? That discrepancy may be changing somewhat: an increasing number of mindfulness teachers are concerned to incorporate social justice issues, and the election of Donald Trump has motivated many Buddhists to become more engaged. Nonetheless, the usual focus of Buddhist practice resonates well with the usual appeal of mindfulness, and both of them accord well with the basic individualism of U.S. society—"What's in it for me?" But are there other factors that encourage this disparity between mindfulness and social engagement? Is there something else integral to the Buddhist traditions that can help us understand the apparent indifference of many Buddhists to the ecological crisis?

Those questions bring us to the deeper, foundational parts of the Buddhist iceberg, usually unnoticed beneath the surface. My point here, as in the previous chapter, is that we don't normally realize the implications of what is below for what is above. We need to examine that relationship if the Buddhist path is to realize its potential in the modern world and become as liberative as we need it to be.

THE CHALLENGE

A few years ago I was reading a fine book by Loyal Rue, titled *Everybody's Story: Wising Up to the Epic of Evolution*, and came across a passage that literally stopped me in my tracks, because it crystallized so well a discomfort with Buddhism (or some types of Buddhism) that had been bothering me. The passage does not refer to Buddhism in particular but to the "Axial Age" religions that originated around the time of the Buddha (the italics are mine):

> The influence of Axial traditions will continue to decline as it becomes ever more apparent that their resources are incommensurate with the moral challenges of the global problematique. In particular, to the extent that these traditions have stressed *cosmological dualism* and *individual salvation* we may say they have encouraged an attitude of indifference toward the integrity of natural and social systems.

Although the language is academic, the claim is clear: insofar as Axial Age traditions (which include Buddhism, Vedanta, Daoism, and Abrahamic religions such as Judaism, Christianity, and Islam) emphasize "cosmological dualism and individual salvation," they encourage indifference to social justice issues and the ecological crisis.

I have considered the implications of this claim at some length in *A New Buddhist Path* and won't repeat that discussion here. Loyal Rue's point is especially relevant to any evaluation of socially engaged Buddhism, however, because it highlights the basic challenge. It's not an insurmountable problem, as we shall see, because the Buddhist tradition is complex and his critique does not apply equally to all its doctrines. Responding to his claim prompts us to distinguish between some incompatible views and helps to clarify the teachings that are most relevant to our situation today.

What Loyal Rue calls "cosmological dualism" is the belief that, in addition to this world, there is another one, usually understood to be better or somehow higher. This is an important aspect of theistic traditions, although they do not necessarily understand that higher reality in the same way. While all of the Abrahamic traditions distinguish God from the world God has created, classical Judaism is more ambiguous about the possibility of eternal postmortem bliss with God in paradise. For Christianity and Islam that possibility is at the core of their religious messages, as commonly understood. If we behave ourselves here, we can hope to go to heaven. The issue is whether that approach makes this world a backdrop to the central drama of human salvation. Does that *goal* devalue one's life in this troubled world into a *means*?

Does Buddhism teach cosmological dualism? That depends on how we understand the relationship between samsara (this world of suffering, craving, and delusion) and nirvana (or *nibbana*, the original Pali term for the Buddhist *summum bonum*). Despite many references to nibbana in the Pali Canon, there remains something unclear about the nature of that goal. Most descriptions are vague metaphors (the shelter, the refuge, and so on) or expressed negatively (the *end* of suffering, craving, delusion). Is nibbana another reality, or a different way of experiencing this world? The Theravada tradition emphasizes *parinibbana*, which is the nibbana attained at death by a fully awakened person who is no longer reborn. Since parinibbana is carefully distinguished from nihilism—the belief that physical death is simply the terminal dissolution of body and mind—the implication seems to be that there must be some postmortem experience, which suggests some other world or dimension of reality. This is also supported by the traditional four stages of enlightenment mentioned in the Pali Canon: the stream-winner, the once-returner (who will be reborn at most one more time), the nonreturner (who is not yet fully enlightened but will not be reborn physically after death), and the arhat (who has attained nibbana). If the nonreturner continues to practice after death, where does he or she reside while doing so?

If nibbana is a place or a state that transcends this world, it is a version of cosmological dualism.

Such a worldview does not necessarily reject social engagement, but it subordinates such engagement into a support for its transcendent goal, as Bhikkhu Bodhi explains:

Despite certain differences, it seems that all forms of classical Buddhism locate the final goal of compassionate action in a transcendent dimension that lies beyond the flux and turmoil of the phenomenal world. For the Mahayana, the transcendent is not absolutely other than phenomenal reality but exists as its inner core. However, just about all classical formulations of the Mahayana, like the Theravada, begin with a devaluation of phenomenal reality in favor of a transcendent state in which spiritual endeavor culminates.

It is for this reason that classical Buddhism confers an essentially *instrumental value* on socially beneficent activity. Such activity can be a contributing cause for the attainment of nibbana or the realization of buddhahood; it can be valued because it helps create better conditions for the moral and meditative life, or because it helps to lead others to the Dharma; but ultimate value, the overriding good, is located in the sphere of transcendent realization. Since socially engaged action pertains to a relatively elementary stage of the path, to the practice of giving or the accumulation of merits, it plays a secondary role in the spiritual life. The primary place belongs to the inner discipline of meditation through which the ultimate good is achieved. And this discipline, to be effective, normally requires a high degree of *social disengagement*. ("Socially Engaged Buddhism and the Trajectory of Buddhist Ethical Consciousness," with original italics)

We notice yet again the duality between means and ends, which will be a recurring theme throughout this book. Bhikkhu Bodhi distinguishes between the Theravada understanding of transcendence, which sharply distinguishes it from our phenomenal world, and the Mahayana perspective, which understands transcendence to be the "inner core" of phenomenal reality. Nevertheless, in his view both traditions begin by devaluing phenomenal reality. The pertinent question is whether "transcending this world" can be understood more metaphorically, as a different way of experiencing (and understanding) this world. Nagarjuna, the most important figure in the Mahayana tradition, famously asserted that there is not even the slightest distinction between samsara and nirvana: the *kotih* (limit or bounds) of nirvana is not different from the *kotih* of samsara. That claim is difficult to reconcile with any goal that prioritizes escape from the physical cycle of repeated birth and death, or transcending phenomenal reality. (I will say more about Nagarjuna's assertion in the next chapter.)

Nagarjuna is widely revered as a founding ancestor of every East Asian Buddhist tradition, including meditatively focused Chan/Zen schools and the more devotionally focused Pure Land schools. I don't remember what, if anything, my Japanese Zen master said about what happens after we die, but he spoke a great deal about the true nature of this world and the importance of realizing that for ourselves with a *kensho* experience (literally, "seeing into one's nature"). In contrast, most Pure Land schools of East Asia emphasize what happens after death: if one has faith in Amitabha Buddha, he will meet us and take us to his western paradise. Conditions in that ideal realm are so perfect that it is relatively easy to practice and attain complete nirvana there—a process that apparently does not involve any further relationship with this world of suffering, craving, and delusion.

In place of a final escape from this world, with no physical rebirth into it, Mahayana traditions such as Chan/Zen emphasize realizing here and now that everything, including us, is *shunya* (Japanese: *ku*), usually translated as "empty." *Shunyata* "emptiness" is thus the transcendent "inner core" of phenomenal reality that Bhikkhu Bodhi refers to. That all things are "empty" means, minimally, that they are not substantial or self-existing, being impermanent phenomena that arise and pass away according to conditions. The implications of this insight for how we engage with the world can be understood in different ways. It is sometimes taken in a nihilistic sense: nothing is real, therefore nothing is important. Seeing everything as illusory discourages social or ecological engagement. Why bother?

The important point here is that "clinging to emptiness" can function in the same way as cosmological dualism, both of them devaluing this world and its problems. Joanna Macy's contribution to *A Buddhist Re-*

sponse to the Climate Emergency identifies this misunderstanding as one of several "spiritual traps that cut the nerve of compassionate action":

> That the phenomenal world is an illusion. Impermanent and made of matter, it is less worthy than a realm of pure spirit. Its pain and its demands on us are less real than the pleasures or tranquility we can find in transcending them.
>
> That suffering is a mistake. Pain we may feel in beholding the world derives from our own cravings and attachments. According to this view, freedom from suffering is attained by non-attachment to the fate of all beings, rather than non-attachment to matters of the ego.
>
> That we create our world unilaterally by the power of our mind. Our subjective thoughts dictate the form things will take. Grief for the plight of the world is negative thinking. Confronting injustice and dangers simply creates more conflict and suffering.
>
> And the corollary, that the world is already perfect when we view it spiritually. We feel then so peaceful that the world will become peaceful without our need to act.

According to Macy, to see this world as illusion is to dwell in an emptiness that is disengaged from its forms, in which the end of suffering involves nonattachment to the fate of beings rather than nonattachment to one's own ego. But the Buddha did not teach—nor does his life demonstrate—that nonattachment means unconcern about what is happening in the world, to the world. When the Heart Sutra famously asserts that "form is not different from emptiness," it immediately adds that "emptiness is not other than form." And forms—including the living beings and ecosystems of this world—suffer.

The Heart Sutra's emphasis on the nonduality of emptiness and form implies a different way of understanding shunyata, which is more than simply asserting that nothing self-exists because everything is dependent on everything else. When we remember Buddhist emphasis on impermanence and insubstantiality, "emptiness" (or "boundlessness," a new translation some teachers prefer) can refer to an *unlimited po-tentiality* that is inherently formless but nonetheless generative, which is why it can become any form according to conditions and changes as those conditions change. Shunyata is not the same as voidness, as Shunryu Suzuki, the founder of San Francisco Zen Center, emphasized: "There is something, but that something is something which is always prepared for taking some particular form. . . ." Our usual way of ex-periencing the world, including ourselves, reifies those impermanent manifestations into supposedly substantial, self-existing objects; en-lightenment involves realizing the "emptiness" of such manifestations.

Explaining this is awkward, because in trying to say something about "it"—this "pure" potentiality, with no characteristics of its own—language inevitably makes this *nothing* into a *something*. Nagarjuna states that to misunderstand shunyata is like grabbing a snake by the wrong end, and the correct view of shunyata is perhaps the most ferociously argued topic in Mahayana philosophy. This is not the place for an overview of that debate, except to point out that such a "potentialist" understanding of shunyata accords well with the dynamic and self-generative *tathagatagarbha* (usually translated as "buddha-nature," but more literally, "buddha womb" or "buddha embryo") described in the Tathagatagarbha Sutras, as well as in the Lotus Sutra, Avatamsaka Sutra, and Lankavatara Sutra, among others. It accords with Dzogchen teachings and is implicit in the *shentong* view of the Jonang school of Tibetan Buddhism, long suppressed by the Gelugpas but recently accepted by eminent masters such as Dilgo Khyentse Rinpoche, Kalu Rinpoche, and Dudjom Rinpoche. And it is consistent with understanding our universe not as a lifeless clock-work mechanism but as an energetic, self-organizing organism, as mentioned in the previous chapter.

For our purposes, understanding shunyata as a formless potential that takes form or "presences" as everything we experience—including ourselves—encourages us *not* to dualize the potential from the ways it presences. This is important because it means that the goal of Buddhist practice is not to dwell serenely in pure possibility (that is, not to "cling to emptiness"), but for our innate potential to manifest in ways that are wise and compassionate, because they contribute to the well-being of its forms—including the manifold species of the biosphere.

Loyal Rue associates the indifference encouraged by cosmological dualism with a focus on individual salvation. In Christianity, for example, whether or not I go to heaven is disconnected from whether or not you go to heaven. Although how I relate to you is very important for my own spiritual destiny, it has no direct effect on yours—that depends on your response. I may sincerely hope that you will go to heaven too and do my best to influence you in a positive way, but at the end of the day—the end of our days—we are separate beings and our ultimate destinies are detached.

Psychologically, at least, there is something disconcerting about this conception of spiritual salvation. All the recent studies I've read about happiness emphasize that the most important factor is the quality of our relationships with others. It is not simply that relationships are important; in a deeper sense, we *are* webs of relationships, just as Indra's Net implies. Death breaks those ties, at least the physical ones, but the notion that an individual attains paradise in being freed from such earthly entanglements reinforces the delusion of a separate self that Buddhism challenges.

Does that mean there is no individual salvation in Buddhism? Buddhists don't aim for heaven: we want to awaken or become enlightened (different terms for the same thing). What enlightenment actually means may not be clear, but it is usually understood to be an individual's experience, discrete from the experience of others. Awakening happens one by one, like Gautama's singular experience under the bodhi tree. You can be enlightened while I am not. You may hope that I will become enlightened too and do what you can to encourage it, yet ultimately your highest well-being—your arhatship or buddhahood—seems to be separate from mine.

Or is it? A counterexample to individual awakening is provided by the bodhisattva path, depending on how we understand that path. According to many traditional accounts, a bodhisattva postpones his or her full enlightenment in order to help others awaken, which seems consistent with the usual view that awakening occurs one by one. But if awakening involves letting go and "forgetting oneself" (as Dogen puts it)—realizing that I am not "inside" separate from the rest of the world "outside"—such nonduality implies that my "salvation" is not disconnected from yours. If I too have no self-existence apart from the world, being interdependent with everything else, how can I be fully awakened unless and until everyone else is too?

To sum up, Loyal Rue's concerns, that cosmological dualism and individual salvation encourage indifference to social and ecological problems, seem to apply to some Buddhist teachings, or at least to some ways of understanding Buddhist teachings, but not to others. Expressed another way, our social and ecological problems encourage us to clarify how Buddhist teachings should be understood today.

A relevant issue, of course, is that contemporary science hasn't discovered anything that supports such cosmological dualisms, Abrahamic or Buddhist. In many other ways Buddhist teachings do seem to accord with modern sensibilities. Emphasis on interdependence is compatible with how ecosystems function. What Buddhism claims about anatta ("not-self") is consistent with what developmental psychology has discovered about the construction of the ego-self. And Buddhist critiques of language—how conceptualizing deceives us—are comparable to a major concern of recent philosophy.

On the other side, however, many educated Buddhists today aren't sure what to believe about a transcendent "otherworldly" reality, or karma as a law of ethical cause-and-effect, or physical rebirth after we die. Some wonder whether awakening too is an outdated myth, similar perhaps to the physical resurrection of Jesus after his crucifixion. So it is not surprising that a more secular, *this-worldly* alternative has become popular, especially in the West: understanding the Buddhist path more psychologically, as a new type of therapy that provides different perspectives on the nature of mental distress and new practices to promote psychological well-being. These include not only reducing greed, ill will, and delusion here and now, but also sorting out our emotional lives and working through personal traumas.

As in psychotherapy, the emphasis of this psychologized Buddhism is on helping us adapt better to the circumstances of our lives. The basic approach is that my main problem is the way my mind works and the solution is to change the way my mind works, so that I can play my various roles (at work, with family, with friends, and so on) better—in short, so that I *fit into this world better*. A common corollary is that the problems we see in the world are projections of our own dissatisfaction with ourselves. According to this spiritual trap, "the world is already perfect when we view it spiritually," as Joanna Macy puts it.

Notice the pattern. Much of traditional Asian Buddhism, especially Theravada Buddhism and the Pali Canon, emphasizes *ending physical rebirth* into this unsatisfactory world. The goal is to escape samsara, this realm of suffering, craving, and delusion that cannot be reformed. In contrast, much of modern Buddhism, especially Buddhist psychotherapy (and most of the mindfulness movement), emphasizes *harmonizing* with this world by transforming one's mind, because one's mind is the problem, not the world. Otherworldly Buddhism and this-worldly Buddhism seem like polar opposites, yet in one important way they agree: neither is much concerned about addressing the problems of this world, to help transform it into a better place. Whether they reject it or embrace it, both take its shortcomings for granted and in that sense accept it for what it is.

Neither approach encourages ecodharma or other types of social engagement. Instead, both encourage a different way of responding to them, which I sometimes facetiously call the Buddhist "solution" to the eco-crisis. By now we're all familiar with the pattern: we read yet another newspaper or online blog reporting on the latest scientific studies, with disheartening ecological implications. Not only are things getting worse, it's happening more quickly than anyone expected. How do we react? The news tends to make us depressed or anxious—but hey, we're Buddhist practitioners, so we know how to deal with that. We meditate for a while, and *our unease about what is happening to the earth goes way* . . . for a while, anyway.

This is not to dismiss the value of meditation, or the relevance of equanimity, or the importance of realizing shunyata. Nevertheless, those by themselves are insufficient as responses to our situation.

Summing up these perspectives—trying to transcend this world or trying to harmonize better with it—we can see that this ambivalence about the nature of awakening is a deep-rooted challenge that contemporary Buddhism can't keep evading. Do the Buddhist path and goal encourage us to engage with social and ecological issues or discourage such engagement as a distraction? To address wholeheartedly the problems that face us today, we really do need to clarify what the essential message is.

DECONSTRUCTING THE SELF

So what is that essential message? Instead of trying to escape this world or fit into it, we can come to experience it, and ourselves, in a different way. This involves deconstructing and reconstructing the individual sense of self, or (more precisely) the relationship between the self and its world. Meditation deconstructs the sense of self, because we "let go" of the habitual patterns of thinking, feeling, and acting that compose it. At the same time, our sense of self is reconstructed in daily life by transforming the most important habitual patterns: our motivations, which affect not only how we relate to other people, but how we actually perceive them and the world generally.

The Tibetan teacher Chögyam Trungpa provided one of the best descriptions of this way of understanding the path and its fruition: "Enlightenment is like falling out of an airplane. The bad news is that there is no parachute. The good news is that there is no ground."

This laconic analogy needs to be to be unpacked. What is the airplane? Why don't we have a parachute? How do we fall out? What does "no ground" mean?

What is the airplane that we fall out of? The airplane is the world we live in, or think we live in: a collection of mostly separate things, including ourselves, in objective space and time. These objects appear at a particular time, change quickly or slowly, and eventually pass out of existence. We usually take this way of experiencing for granted, as just the way the world is, but it is a collective construct that we are socialized into as we grew up. We learn to see the world in the same way that those around us do (in large part due to language, which will be discussed in the next chapter).

Although this "consensus reality" is not just an illusion, it is not real in the way we ordinarily assume. Ram Dass calls it "relatively real." Mahayana philosophy distinguishes this conventional or phenomenal reality (as Bhikkhu Bodhi, among others, terms it) from absolute or ultimate reality. It's like the two sides of a hand. The back of your hand—what you see when you make a fist—corresponds to the conventional understanding. Usually we perceive only the fist, so the initial task is to become aware of the palm; but that does not mean the fist is an illusion to be rejected. To extend the metaphor, it is important to know how to use both the palm and the fist, and when.

> Your hand opens and closes and opens and closes.
> If it were always a fist or always stretched open,
> You would be paralyzed.
> (Rumi)

The problem with conventional reality is that it can't fully satisfy us. It involves suffering. In addition to the cravings and pains of our easily injured bodies, life in the phenomenal world is haunted by old age, illness, and death, as highlighted in the mythic story of the Buddha's own life. Human self-consciousness means we know not only that we are alive, but that we won't always be alive. As someone put it, there are only two kinds of people: those who are dead and those who will soon be dead.

The prince who was to become Buddha left home because he was shocked to see an old man, a sick man, and then a corpse, which triggered an existential crisis as he became aware of the destiny of all human beings, including himself. After his awakening under the bodhi tree, he taught for many years. Eventually he became old, with back pain and stomach problems, and then he died. So in what way did he solve the problem?

He solved it by not being physically reborn back into this world of samsara, according to the Theravada tradition. But there is another way to understand what happened, which emphasizes the nibbana that occurred under the bodhi tree more than the parinibbana when he finally passed away. Old age, illness, and death are aspects of the phenomenal world—the fist—and his enlightenment revealed the palm: that aging, being ill, and dying are "empty" insofar as there is no substantial self that experiences them.

Physical and mental pains are forms of suffering, and so is inability to satisfy one's cravings, and so is realizing our mortality. Yet the most troublesome dukkha of all haunts the delusion of a self *inside*— behind the eyes, perhaps, or between the ears—that believes itself to be separate from the rest of the world *outside*. That the world we normally take for granted is a construct means not only that the appearances we perceive are reified into self-existing *objects*; it means that habitual ways of thinking, perceiving, feeling, acting, reacting, remembering, intending, and so forth are reified into a self-existing *subject*. Because this supposedly separate self is actually insubstantial, a cluster of mental and physical processes rather than something real, it is inherently insecure. It can never secure itself because there is nothing that could be secured. As Gertrude Stein might say, there is no there there.

Although this understanding of the self may seem theoretical, the consequences are not. We usually experience this insecurity as a sense of *lack*: the feeling that something is wrong with me, that *I am not good enough*, which becomes personalized in different ways. We all have this sense of lack, but normally each of us understands it as his or her own particular problem, rather than being inherent to the (unenlightened) human condition. Another way to describe this situation is that there is a tension between what I think I am (*some*-thing substantial and real) and what I feel or sense that I am (*no*-thing).

This generates *what I should be . . .* , a self-image that we never quite measure up to.

The world as a collection of supposedly real, self-existing things, including myself, is haunted by dukkha. That is the airplane we must fall out of.

Why don't we have a parachute? Parachutes are what keep us from plummeting into the abyss. Because the sense of self is always insecure, it always tries to identify with something, as a way to ground itself. We become preoccupied with what might be called *lack projects* (trying to fill up our sense of lack) or *reality projects* (trying to become or feel more real). These projects take various forms. Many of them are *if onlys* . . . "If only I had enough money . . . consumer toys . . . a car . . . a better car . . . a partner . . . a better partner . . ." They are not always objects: "If only I were more famous . . . more intelligent . . . more powerful . . . more attractive . . ." In a commencement address at Kenyon College (now published as the book *This Is Water*), the novelist David Foster Wallace described these as things we worship:

> In the day-to-day trenches of adult life, there is actually no such thing as atheism. There is no such thing as not worshipping. Everybody worships. The only choice we get is *what* to worship. And an outstanding reason for choosing some sort of God or spiritual-type thing to worship . . . is that pretty much anything else you worship will eat you alive. If you worship money and things—if they are where you tap real meaning in life—then you will never have enough. Never feel you have enough. It's the truth. Worship your own body and beauty and sexual allure and you will always feel ugly, and when time and age start showing, you will die a million deaths before they finally plant you. . . . Worship power—you will feel weak and afraid, and you will need ever more power over others to keep the fear at bay. Worship your intellect, being seen as smart— you will end up feeling stupid, a fraud, always on the verge of being found out. And so on.

Worship is a good term for these lack projects, for they are sacred inasmuch as they are at the heart of our self-understanding, including the meaning of our lives and our role in the world. Unfortunately, they don't work as solutions to our sense of lack, because one is looking in the wrong place. Such projects are symptoms of a deeper problem. We seek the answer outside ourselves, yet the basic difficulty is inside: an insecure sense of self that can never secure itself by identifying with something, a constructed self that can never feel real enough.

Inside the airplane, however, conditioned by our upbringing and culture, we take these obsessions for granted. They are what everyone worships, aspects of conventional reality built into the way society is organized. We normally don't realize there are other options. Wallace continues:

> Look, the insidious thing about these forms of worship is not that they're evil or sinful; it is that they are *unconscious*. They are default-settings. They're the kind of worship you just gradually slip into, day after day, getting more and more selective about what you see and how you measure value without ever being fully aware that that's what you're doing. And the world will not discourage you from operating on your default-settings, because the world of men and money and power hums along quite nicely on the fuel of fear and contempt and frustration and craving and the worship of self.

David Foster Wallace was not, as far as I know, interested in Buddhism or meditation, but he understood that the alternative to such idols "involves attention, and awareness, and discipline, and effort, and being able truly to care about other people and to sacrifice for them, over and over, in myriad petty little unsexy ways, every day."

One form of worship that Wallace does not mention is attachment to charismatic people, who attract us because they seem not to suffer from the sense of lack that bothers us so much. Such figures appear to be larger than life—more *real* than the rest of us—which fascinates us in ways that are often problematic (Hitler, Mao) but can be positive (Gandhi, the Dalai Lama). Tellingly, Ernest Becker's great book *The Denial of Death* has a chapter titled "The Spell Cast by Persons—The Nexus of Unfreedom." Perhaps we are so susceptible because of our species' uniquely long childhood, which makes us more dependent on authority figures; the need to find security by subjecting ourselves to others persists in the ways we make them into heroes and want to participate in their aura. Politicians such as Ronald Reagan and Donald Trump exploit this propensity, and the media have learned how to commodify it by creating pop stars and movie idols. Is the religious aspiration for a messiah, who will eventually appear to save us from ourselves, another version of the same tendency?

Of course, this has important implications for why we put Zen masters, rinpoches, and other gurus on pedestals, seeing them as superhuman. Is it that they are in fact so special, or is this more a function of our need to see them as special? This projection can be beneficial: we are inspired by their example to become more like them, or more like what we think they are. Problems occur when the teacher gets caught up in the countertransference: when you are surrounded by students who think that you are godlike, it is tempting to agree with them. Sooner or later the projection needs to be broken, to realize that the master too is all too human. This is often painful, but if it doesn't happen, the student remains spiritually immature. If it happens too soon—because the teacher acts badly, for example—it can destroy the student's practice. If it happens at the right time, students are ready because they have realized their own buddha-nature.

There are other things we identify with, which involve trying to secure the self by trying to stabilize its world. I am not sure whether to label them as lack projects, but some of them amount to the same thing: for example, we often find meaning by associating with certain groups in opposition to other groups, hence the appeal of racism and nationalism. We also become attached to particular worldviews. The Buddha had quite a bit to say about this. In the Samma-Ditthi Sutta he identified views (*ditthi*) as one of the four types of clinging that we should let go of (the others are sensual pleasures, rules and rituals, and belief in the self as something substantial). The parable of the raft applies this to his own teachings. The Dharma is for helping us "cross over" to the other side, not something to be embraced as salvific in and of itself—like a raft carried around on one's back after crossing a river. Buddhist teachings are not sacred but guidebooks or road maps to help us go somewhere.

Can attachment to certain people (teachers) and views (the Dharma) make the Buddhist path into a lack project/reality project (which will make us special)? Something like that may be unavoidable at the beginning, and perhaps that is not altogether a bad thing. Or, to say it another way, the Buddhist path is a "lack project," but one that can actually resolve the problem: not by filling up the sense of lack, but by deconstructing the sense of self that it shadows.

In other words, Buddhism is a path that, if all goes well, deconstructs itself. Although Buddhism can be a marker of ethnic or cultural identity, one more thing to cling to, meditation tends to undermine such dualistic affiliations: "I'm a Buddhist, not a . . ." There is nothing liberative about such labels. The important thing is whether or not one is a practitioner. Ironically, we discover what we seek by opening up to the groundlessness we have been fleeing.

How do we fall out of the airplane? The issue here is: do I jump or am I pushed? That is, is enlightenment something that the sense of self *does* or something that happens to it? Insofar as awakening means realizing what I have always been—that there is nothing to gain, because the self has always been "empty"—this is, once again, the familiar problem of means versus ends. The irony is that we strive to attain something that cannot be attained, because it's not something we have ever really lacked.

This tension has been a crucial issue in many religious traditions, although conceptualized in different ways. Within Japanese Zen, for example, it is the difference between Rinzai and Soto. Rinzai practice uses intensive meditation retreats to experience kensho, a taste or glimpse of enlightenment, like a general who marshals all his troops and charges into the battlefield. In contrast, the Soto practice of *shikan taza*, "just sitting," accords with Dogen's emphasis that meditation itself already manifests the "empty" mind of enlightenment, whether we have realized it or not yet. This approach is like a farmer who patiently plants his rice seedlings, one by one. The Rinzai approach can dualize the means from the goal, "grasping at not-grasping," while the Soto approach can foster a complacency that loses the importance of actually awakening to our true nature.

The same tension recurs in the difference between Zen generally, which emphasizes *jiriki*, "self-power," and the more devotional Pure Land schools, which emphasize *tariki*, "other-power." Zen practitioners are encouraged to meditate, while Pure Land devotees cultivate faith that after they die Amida Buddha will escort them to his Pure Land.

Hindu Vedanta makes a similar distinction between monkey-liberation and cat-liberation. A baby monkey must cling to its mother's breast as she swings from tree to tree, but a kitten does not need to do anything, because its mother picks it up by the scruff of the neck and carries it where she will. Do we need to perform practices to reach the Divine, or does the Divine embrace us if and when it wants to?

So which is it? According to an aphorism sometimes attributed to Shunryu Suzuki, "Enlightenment is always an accident, but meditation makes us accident-prone." There is no straightforward cause-and-effect relationship between meditation and enlightenment. Meditation is letting go of the habitual thought-patterns that compose the sense of self, which involves some effort on our part. Awakening, however, happens in its own time. The self can't do it because it's what happens to that sense of self. According to my teacher Yamada Koun, "There's no greater service we can do on this earth than to let the ego diminish in zazen, so that the infinite life within us has a chance to take over." Zazen does not cause that infinite life to take over, but the odds improve considerably. Although Dogen recommends "forgetting the self," that's not something we can willfully do—so we approach it indirectly. As Yamada also said, practice is about forgetting yourself in the act of uniting (or becoming one) with something, as happens when we work on a koan such as *Mu*. As we repeat that sound indefinitely, the sense of a self that is *doing* it becomes more and more attenuated.

As one's meditation practice matures, some practitioners feel as if they are on the edge of an abyss. You may sense that all you need to do is let go of yourself, yet you can't do it. Instead you tense up and contract. Here the teacher can help, sometimes with a few words, sometimes with an abrupt, unexpected action such as a shout or a blow, which can startle the student into letting go. But the student must be ripe.

> "The Dharma is not a secure refuge. He who enjoys a secure refuge is not interested in the Dharma, but in a secure refuge." (Vimalakirti Sutra)

What does "no ground" mean? We need to "boldly let go on the edge of the cliff . . . you only revive after death" (in the words of Chan master Boshan). "Die before you die," as a Sufi saying puts it, "so that when it comes time to die you are already dead."

An earlier Chan master, Huangbo, explains (as translated by John Blofeld): "Men are afraid to forget their minds, fearing to fall through the Void with nothing to stay [stop] their fall. They do not know that the Void is not really Void, but the realm of the real Dharma." Elsewhere he elaborates: "Many people are afraid to empty their minds lest they may plunge into the Void. They do not know that their own Mind *is* the void."

One doesn't really fall but lets go, opens up to . . . what? The important point is that the Void Huangbo mentions is not something that grounds the sense of self but a groundlessness where there's no security or insecurity because there's no self that needs to be secured. It turns out that the true nature of the self, one's own true nature, lacks nothing because it *is* nothing—or, better, is *no-thing*. Realizing this liberates me to become this, to do that, according to the situation, because I am no longer motivated by a misconstrued obsession to become more real.

What was said earlier about shunyata emptiness also applies to what Yamada Koun calls our essential nature—because they are the same thing. Commenting on a koan in *The Gateless Gate*, he emphasizes that every one of us is

> one with the whole universe. At the same time, every one of us is extremely poor, for in our essential nature there is nothing. There is neither subject nor object. There is nothing to be seen, to be touched, to be handled. It has no form, no color, no weight, *no place to stay*. In a word, our essential nature is totally void. On the other hand, this void has limitless treasures. It can see, it can hear, it can cry, it can laugh, run, eat. In a word, it is limitless. Emptiness and limitlessness are characteristics of our essential nature.

One of the greatest Chan masters, Linji, emphasized the same thing. "If you want to be free to be born or die, to go or stay as one would put on or take off a garment, then you must understand right now that the person here listening to the Dharma [you!] has no form, no characteristics, no root, no beginning, no place he abides, yet he is vibrantly alive. . . . That is what I call the secret of the matter."

No place to stay, no place he abides: the separate sense of self cannot ground itself, but when we realize our true nature, there is no need to do so. Groundlessness turns out to be as much of a ground as we need. "Miraculously, everything is radically transformed though remaining just as it is" (Yasutani Haku'un).

Letting go and opening up to this groundlessness is to experience what cannot die insofar as it was never born. In the consensus reality of the airplane, you and I are two more objects in the world, born at a certain time and dying sometime later. From this other perspective, however, we (like everything else) have always been impermanent manifestations of something formless, nameless, and limitless. The ways that this ungraspable no-thing-ness manifests arise and pass away, but that which temporarily manifests as these forms and names does not pass away.

Buddhist literature includes many references to "the unborn," which is another term for our essential nature. Passages in the Pali Canon emphasize that "the sage who is at peace is not born, does not age, does not die; he is not shaken and is not agitated. For there is nothing present in him by which he might be born. Not being born, how could he age? Not aging, how could he die? Not dying, how could he be shaken?" (Dhatuvibhanga Sutta).

Perhaps the most famous example is in the Udana Sutta:

> There is, O monks, an unborn, an unbecome, an unmade, an unfabricated; if, O monks, there were not here this unborn, unbecome, unmade, unfabricated, there would not be here an escape from the born, the become, the made, the fabricated. But because there is an unborn . . . therefore there is an escape from the born.

Such passages are often understood to describe what happens after a fully awakened person physically dies: he or she is not reborn. Mahayana teachings are more explicit that the "unborn" refers to an aspect of shunyata that applies here and now. The Heart Sutra explains that all things are shunya because they are "not created and not annihilated," which is why "there is no old age and death." Nagarjuna echoes this in the prefatory verse to his *Mulamadhyamakakarika*, the most important work of Mahayana philosophy, which says that the true nature of things is that they do not die and they are not born, they do not cease to be and they are not eternal.

In Chinese Buddhism the "Song of Enlightenment" of Yongjia Xuanjue, a disciple of the sixth Chan Patriarch, declares that "since I abruptly realized the unborn, I have had no reason for joy or sorrow at any honor or disgrace." No one, however, emphasized the unborn more than the beloved seventeenth-century Japanese Zen master Bankei, for whom it was his central teaching. "When you dwell in the Unborn itself, you're dwelling at the very wellhead of buddhas and ancestors." Being our essential nature, the Unborn is not something that can be gained. "It's wrong for you to breed a second mind on top of the mind you already have by trying to *become* the Unborn. You're unborn right from the start. . . . The true Unborn has nothing to do with fundamental principles and it's beyond becoming or attaining. It's simply *being who you are*." A visiting monk asked Bankei, "What happens when someone who believes in the Unborn dies? Is he born again or not?" He responded: "At the place of the Unborn, there's no distinction between being born and not being born."

There is no distinction between being born and not being born, because such characteristics do not apply to that which has no characteristics, which is the true "empty" nature of our minds.

This is where some teachings end, but when we understand shunyata as "unlimited potentiality" and remember the heart of the Heart Sutra ("form does not differ from emptiness, emptiness is not different from form"), we realize that realizing the unborn, by itself, is insufficient. Emptiness is not a place to dwell, because it is not a place, as Linji and Yamada Koun both emphasize. I also remember Yamada Roshi emphasizing that a genuine kensho is accompanied by the spontaneous uprising of compassion. "When you recognize the empty nature, the energy to benefit others dawns, effortless and un-contrived," as Dilgo Khyentse expressed it. The ultimate fruit of the path is described in the last of the ten oxherding pictures: returning to the marketplace with helping hands.

Awakening to the unborn is incomplete because deconstruction of the constructed sense of self does not automatically transform how we relate to people. Our deep-rooted and usually self-preoccupied ha-bitual ways of thinking, feeling, and acting tend to have a life of their own, which means that a gradual *reconstruction* of how we actually live in the world is also necessary. The "three poisons" of greed, ill will, and delusion need to be transmuted into more positive motivations: generosity, loving-kindness (or basic friendliness), and the wisdom that recognizes my well-being is not separate from your well-being or from that of the earth itself. Discussing reconstruction after de-construction suggests that the one happens after the other, but these processes occur together and support each other. Meditation helps us be more mindful in daily life, thus more aware of our motivations and less likely to react in a problematic way.

SELFLESS ENGAGEMENT

So what does all this have to do with ecological engagement? In order to comprehend what Buddhism can contribute to understanding and responding to the eco-crisis, it has been important to clarify what the spiritual path involves, in language avoiding the cosmological dualism that Loyal Rue critiques. If we view the ultimate goal as escaping from this world—whether the end of rebirth or dwelling in an emptiness indifferent to its forms and therefore immune to its troubles—or as simply harmonizing with the world and its institutions, then we are unlikely to engage fully with the social and ecological challenges that call out to us today.

One of my favorite Zen koans speaks to this. A student asks the master: "What is the constant activity of all the buddhas and bodhisattvas?"—what is special about how enlightened people live, moment by moment? Perhaps the student was wondering if they manifest some extraordinary powers. The master's reply is short and simple: "Responding appropriately." That's all.

How wonderful! But in order to respond appropriately, we need to understand our situation. In a Zen monastery it's easy to know what's appropriate: when the bell rings we put on our robes and go to the practice hall to meditate. But what about when we leave the monastery grounds and reenter the wider world, with its social and ecological problems? Realizing that our essential groundlessness is an inexhaustible potential enables us to respond appropriately to them.

Gandhi famously said that our greatness as human beings lies not so much in being able to remake the world as in being able to remake ourselves—but are those transformations really so independent? His own example suggests not. As we begin to wake up and realize that we are not separate from each other, nor from this wondrous earth, we realize that the ways we live together and relate to the earth need to be reconstructed too. That means not only social engagement as individuals helping other individuals, but finding ways to address the problematic economic and political structures that are deeply implicated in the eco-crisis and the social justice issues that confront us today. This reclaims the goal of enlightenment from an exclusively individualistic model. Engagement in the world is how our personal awakening blossoms, and contemplative practices such as meditation ground our activism, transforming it into a spiritual path.

Walk as if you are kissing the Earth with your feet.

—THICH NHAT HANH

The faster we live, the less emotion is left in the world. The slower we live, the deeper we feel the world around us.

—STANKO ABADŽIĆ

The child of a certain rabbi used to wander in the woods. At first his father let him wander, but over time he became concerned. One day he said to his son, "You know, I have noticed that each day you walk into the woods. I wonder why you go there?" The boy answered, "I go there to find God." "That is a very good thing," the father replied gently. "I am glad you are searching for God. But, my child, don't you know that God is the same everywhere?" Yes," the boy answered, "but I'm not."

—RICHARD LOUV

Before, nature had a life and spirit of its own. The trees, skies, and rivers were living spirits. Now we are only concerned with how they can serve us.

—PHRA PAISAL WISALO

We need to lose the world, to lose a world, and to discover there is more than one world and that the world isn't what we think it is.

—HELENE CIXOUS

I do not reject the present moment to pursue what time will bring. I reject what time will bring to pursue the present moment.

—SAMIDDHI SUTTA

Real generosity to the future lies in giving all to the present.

—ALBERT CAMUS

When I think of all the books I have read, and of the wise words I have heard spoken, and of the anxiety I have given to parents and grandparents, and of the hopes I have had, all life weighed in the scales of my own life seems to me a preparation for something that never happens.

—WILLIAM BUTLER YEATS

Half our life is spent trying to find something to do with the time we have rushed through life trying to save.

—WILL ROGERS

When we oppose things that are too efficient, we mustn't try to be even more efficient. For that will not turn out to be the most efficient way.

—JACQUES ELLUL

When a behavior becomes the norm, we lose our ability to view it as dysfunctional.

—JEFF GARSON

The rose is without *why*, it blooms simply because it blooms. It pays no attention to itself, nor does it ask whether anyone sees it.

—ANGELUS SILESIUS

We have deprived nature of its independence, and this is fatal to its meaning. Nature's independence *is its meaning*—without it there is nothing but us.

—BILL MCKIBBEN

It is not what we do that makes us holy, but we should make holy what we do.

—MEISTER ECKHART

There is no bifurcation in reality between the human and the
non-human realms.

—Warwick Fox

The Western version of mystical awareness, our version of Buddhism
or Taoism, will be ecological awareness.

—Fritjof Capra

There is as yet no ethic dealing with man's relation to land and to
the animals and plants which grow upon it. . . . The land-relation is
still strictly economic, entailing privileges but not obligations. The
extension of ethics to this third element in human environment is,
if I read the evidence correctly, an evolutionary possibility and an
ecological necessity.

—Aldo Leopold

Sooner or later, we will have to realize that the earth has rights, too,
to live without pollution.

—Bolivian president Evo Morales

3

What Are
We Overlooking?

ACCORDING TO TRADITIONAL biographies, Gautama Buddha had a special relationship with trees.

He was born among trees in Lumbini Grove, when his mother went into premature labor. As a child, while sitting under a tree and watching his father plow a field as part of a religious ceremony, he spontaneously entered a meditative trance. Later, when he left home on his spiritual quest, he went into the forest where he studied with two teachers, engaged in ascetic practices, and then meditated by himself under a tree—where he awakened. Afterward he continued to spend most of his time outdoors, often teaching under trees and eventually dying between two trees.

Unsurprisingly, the Buddha often expressed his appreciation of trees and other plants. According to one story in the Vinaya monastic code, a tree spirit appeared to him and complained that a monk had chopped down its tree. In response, the Buddha prohibited sangha members from damaging trees or bushes, including cutting off limbs, picking flowers, or even plucking green leaves. One wonders what he would say about our casual destruction of whole ecosystems.

We may also wonder about the larger pattern: why religious founders so often experience their spiritual transformation by leaving human society and going into the wilderness. Following his own

baptism, Jesus went into the desert where he fasted for forty days
and nights by himself. Muhammad's revelations occurred when he
retreated into a cave, where he was visited by the archangel Gabriel.
The Khaggavisana ("Rhinoceros Horn") Sutta, one of the earliest in
the Pali Canon, encourages monks to wander alone in the forest, like
a rhinoceros. Milarepa, and many Tibetan yogis since him, lived and
practiced in a cave by himself for many years. Today, in contrast, most
of us meditate inside buildings with screened windows, which insulate us from insects, the hot sun, and chilling winds. There are many
advantages to this, of course—but is something significant lost?

Although we often view nature in a utilitarian way, the natural
world is an interdependent community of living beings that invites
us into a different kind of relationship. The implication is that withdrawing into it, especially by oneself, can disrupt our usual ways of
seeing and open us up to an alternative experience. Understanding
more about how that happens may also give us deeper insight into
what is problematic about our present collective relationship with the
natural world.

In order to gain that understanding, however, let us first consider a
puzzle presented by some different Buddhist teachings. This will also
clarify some of the points made in the previous chapter.

CRAVING VERSUS CONCEPTUALIZING

From the beginning Buddhism has emphasized dukkha—"suffering"
in the broadest sense. The Buddha said that what he had to teach was
dukkha and how to end it. Why do we suffer? According to the second
of the four noble (or ennobling) truths, the cause of dukkha is *tanha,*
usually translated as "desire" or "craving," yet etymologically closer to
"thirst." Tanha is not a thirst for anything in particular but a thirst for
everything, because nothing can satisfy it.

Yet I do not remember my Zen teacher, Yamada Koun, mentioning that the problem is craving; for that matter, I do not recall him
ever referring to the four noble truths. For the Zen tradition, and

Mahayana generally, what is most problematic is related to conceptualizing, which deludes us.

Pali texts and Theravada Buddhists also talk about delusion, for clinging to certain types of thinking can be understood as a form of craving—but the difference in emphasis is nonetheless striking. Is our primary problem craving or delusion? How can we understand the relationship between them? Are early Buddhism and Zen even talking about the same path, the same enlightenment?

The difficulty here is that something is missing, which is needed to connect craving with delusive concepts. To find that missing link, let's return to Nagarjuna's great philosophical treatise the *Mulamadhyamakakarika*. According to the earliest Buddhist texts, the goal of the Buddhist path is to transcend samsara—our everyday world of suffering, craving, and delusion—by attaining nirvana and not being reborn. In the previous chapter, however, I quoted Nagarjuna's famous assertion that there is no distinction between those. "The limit [kotih] of nirvana is also the limit of everyday life. There is not even the slightest difference between them." This denies any cosmological dualism. The "consensus reality" we normally take for granted is in fact a psychological and social construction that can be deconstructed and reconstructed. But we still need to know more about how that construct functions in our everyday lives. How do craving and conceptualizing work together to fabricate a world composed of apparently separate objects that occasionally interact "in" objective space and time? To explain that, something else in needed.

In the final verse of the same nirvana chapter Nagarjuna points out the missing third term. As translated by Mervyn Sprung, "Ultimate serenity [shiva] is the coming to rest of all ways of taking things, the repose of named things; no truth [Dharma] has been taught by a Buddha for anyone, anywhere." From the highest point of view the Buddha taught nothing because awakening does not involve conceptually grasping anything: it is *the repose of named things*.

We perceive this world as samsara because we *grasp* it. Grasping at things reifies them into objects. When we don't grasp at things, we can experience them (and ourselves) quite differently. So the important question is, how do we grasp the world? Nagarjuna's verse implies that it has something to do with naming things.

The essential point is something counterintuitive. We normally believe that we see things and then label them with names, as if language were transparent or a mirror reflecting things as they are. But it doesn't work like that. Learning to talk plays a big role in how we construct the world. It's part of the socialization process. When children learn a language, they are learning to perceive the world (including themselves) in the same way that other language-speakers do. The philosopher John Searle says it well:

> When we experience the world we experience it through linguistic categories that help to shape the experiences themselves. The world doesn't come to us already sliced up into objects and experiences. What counts as an object is already a function of our system of representation [i.e., language], and how we experience the world is influenced by that system of representation.

As psychologists have discovered, we don't normally look that closely at things. "Perception seems to be a matter of looking up information that has been stored about objects and how they behave in various situations. The retinal image does little more than select the relevant stored data" (Richard Gregory). A little glimpse is all we need to perceive something *as* a "cup"—in a sense, we *think* with the eyes. This is not a conscious process but a preconscious one that is usually quite difficult not to do.

Buddhist emphasis on the impermanence of everything implies that the world is a confluence of interacting processes, but due to language we *perceive* it as a collection of separate things—each with its own name—that occasionally interact.

As we begin to speak, we learn to recognize things—Mommy, Daddy, bed, water, toilet, cup, spoon, and so forth—and we also learn

verbs that describe activities—eat, drink, wash, go to bed and so on—
and that brings us to the crucial point, the missing term that links
craving (intentions) and delusion (concepts). A cup, for example, isn't
just a label that identifies a certain type of thing. It's a concept that has
a *function* built into it. To see something *as* a cup is to know what that
thing is used for. The function is preconsciously built into what we
perceive, which is why, moving around the kitchen, I don't perceive
things *as* forks, cups, and plates. I see forks, cups, and plates—various
utensils to be used in different ways. Although I've learned to see the
kitchen that way, the fact that I've learned to see it that way is not
something I'm normally aware of.

That is how concepts organize the world for us: with language we
learn to experience the world in much the same way that our fellow
language-speakers do. But there is one more vital point. Seeing my
world largely as a collection of utensils connects it with my intentions. It enables me to satisfy my desires. If I'm a chocoholic, being
able to identify something as a chocolate bar becomes important.
That identification is connected with many other concepts, functions,
and intentions: knowing where I can buy a chocolate bar, what to do
when I get there, what money is . . . lots of causes and conditions need
to be understood and met for me to enjoy that chocolate bar. Usually,
however, this complex sequence is automatized, so that we don't need
to think much about it. I just go buy the chocolate bar and eat it.

To sum up, three things work together to construct our world: *language* (concepts), which not only divides up the world but organizes
it into *functions* (causal relationships), and the way those functions
enable us to *act intentionally* (e.g., to satisfy desires).

Of the many things that are labeled, one in particular stands out:
me. The self. *I* am not the one doing this construction, for the sense of
self is one of the things constructed. Subjectivity is the first thing to be
"objectified." Learning to use words such as *I*, *me*, and *mine* is learning
to understand oneself as one of the objects that is "in" the world—
another thing that is born and dies, or is created and destroyed—in
much the same way that everything else is. This is actually quite odd

because "I" am essential to "my" world in a way that nothing else ever can be.

The important point here is that learning to see the world as a collection of utensils, used to satisfy my desires, is what constructs the sense of separation between me "inside" (the one who uses things) and the rest of the world "outside" (the things that are used). The act of *grasping* creates both the *grasper* and the *grasped,* which arise in relation to each other. And, as the last chapter discussed, this constructed sense of separation is inherently uncomfortable, creating a self that can never secure itself, because that supposed self is a fiction created by grasping.

Nevertheless, the usual way of experiencing the world (including oneself), and the usual way of living in that world, are not "bad." In fact, they are necessary. This collective construction or "consensus reality" has been indispensable for our evolutionary ability to survive and thrive, and knowing how to function within such a construct remains essential in our daily lives and interactions with other people. The problem is that we normally and unconsciously accept this way of understanding the world as the way things really are, unaware it's a psychosocial construct that can be deconstructed. Rather than identify with it or reject it, what's important is realizing that there is another way of experiencing the world and being able to move freely from one way to the other, "responding appropriately" according to circumstances.

When we experience life only as an incessant succession of intentions and desires, which keeps us grasping the world as a collection of utensils, then we are constantly overlooking something important about it that William Blake famously described in *The Marriage of Heaven and Hell*:

> If the doors of perception were cleansed every thing would
> appear to man as it is, infinite. For man has closed himself up,
> till he sees all things thro' narrow chinks of his cavern.

Clinging to concepts, functions, and cravings is how we close ourselves up. Letting go of them is how the doors of our perceptions become cleansed. Blake also referred to this different way of perceiving in *Auguries of Innocence*:

> To see the world in a grain of sand
> And a heaven in a wild flower
> Hold infinity in the palm of your hand
> And eternity in an hour.

As Blake's reference to eternity suggests, the problem with being stuck in a world of concepts, functions, and cravings can also be expressed in terms of time. When we perceive the world primarily as a collection of utensils, which we grasp in order to chase after what we desire, we are also instrumentalizing the present into a means to achieve something in the future. The present becomes devalued into a series of moments that fall away, as we reach for something that is not yet. The sense of self's sense of *lack* means that the present can never be good enough. Our *lack* projects are always future-oriented. Again, to do this is to overlook something about right now, what is sometimes called the *eternal now*: not the present as an infinitesimal dividing line between the infinities of past and future, but a present that is "without end or beginning" (the literal meaning of eternal). Such a present does not fall away because it lacks nothing.

Is this why we delight in the innocence of children and pets, why we appreciate music and dance so much? In an over-instrumentalized world, they bring us back to the here and now. Young children, in particular, haven't learned yet that life is a serious business and that they need to start always preparing for the future. Perhaps Jesus was alluding to that when he declared: "Truly I tell you, unless you change and become like little children, you will never enter the kingdom of heaven." Maybe the kingdom of heaven is closer than we realize.

Does this also explain why we enjoy being in nature so much? We find it healing, even when we don't understand why or how, but clearly it has something to do with the fact that the natural world offers us a temporary escape from our instrumentalized lives.

Preconsciously constructing the world with language traps us within language. Because meaning for us has become a function of words, we tend to miss the meaning of everything else. In *A Language Older than Words,* Christopher Manes contrasts this with our earlier experience:

> For most cultures throughout history—including our own in preliterate times—the entire world used to speak. Anthropologists call this animism, the most pervasive worldview in human history. Animistic cultures listen to the natural world. For them, birds have something to say. So do worms, wolves, and waterfalls.

They have not ceased to speak but we are no longer able to hear what they are saying.

In *The Re-Enchantment of the World,* Morris Berman elaborates this point:

> The view of nature which predominated in the West down to the eve of the Scientific Revolution was that of an enchanted world. Rocks, trees, rivers, and clouds were all seen as wondrous, alive, and human beings felt at home in this environment. The cosmos, in short, was a place of belonging. A member of this cosmos was not an alienated observer of it but a direct participant in its drama. His personal destiny was bound up with its destiny, and this relationship gave meaning to his life. This type of consciousness . . . involves merger, or identification, with one's surroundings, and bespeaks a psychic wholeness that has long since passed from the scene.

For many indigenous peoples still "there are not two worlds, of persons (society) and things (nature), but just one world—one environment—saturated with personal powers and embracing both human beings, the animals and plants on which they depend, and the landscape in which they live and move" (Tim Ingold).

A classic example is provided in *Lame Deer: Seeker of Visions,* when the Lakota Indian Lame Deer calls the attention of a visitor to his cooking pot:

It doesn't seem to have a message, that old pot, and I guess you don't give it a thought. . . . But I'm an Indian. I think about ordinary, common things like this pot. The bubbling water comes from the rain cloud. It represents the sky. The fire comes from the sun which warms us all—men, animals, trees. The meat stands for the four-legged creatures, our animal brothers, who gave of themselves so that we should live. The steam is living breath. It was water; now it goes up to the sky, becomes a cloud again. These things are sacred. . . . We Sioux spend a lot of time thinking about everyday things. . . . We see in the world around us many symbols that teach us the meaning of life. We have a saying that the white man sees so little, he must see with only one eye. We see a lot that you no longer notice. You could notice if you wanted to, but you are usually too busy. We Indians live in a world of symbols and images where the spiritual and the commonplace are one.

Notice that this extraordinary passage implies no cosmological dualism, although "a world of symbols and images" can be a bit misleading. Lame Deer is describing a different way of *perceiving* the world. His old pot is more than a utensil. For him cooking dinner is a sacred act, because he does not overlook the enchanted cosmos that he participates in.

These references to other spiritual traditions remind us that Buddhism does not have a monopoly on the Dharma. The other nondual tradition that resonates most deeply with the perspective offered in this book is Daoism. This should not surprise us, given the ways that Daoism interacted with Mahayana Buddhism in China, but Daoism is also the Axial Age tradition that most emphatically roots itself in the natural world. Nagarjuna's claim that samsara is not different from nirvana was nothing new to China, which had little interest in any awakening that bifurcates us from this world.

In Daoism's two most important texts, the *Daodejing* and especially the *Zhuangzi*, nature is not only a refuge but reveals the true nature of things, which human civilization tends to obscure. Both turn their backs on society in order to commune with forests and mountains and their creatures. The Dao does not transcend this world, for it is an empty and inexhaustible no-thing-ness that gives birth to all its ten thousand things, and becoming no-thing is a return to that source. In fact, if Buddhist shunyata is understood as a limitless potential without any forms or characteristics of its own, generating all the forms we experience, then it becomes difficult to distinguish shunyata from the Dao. As the *Zhuangzi* says:

> There is somewhere from which we are born, into which we die, from which we come forth, through which we go in; it is this that is called the Gate of Heaven. The Gate of Heaven is that which is without anything; the myriad things go on coming forth from that which is without anything. Something cannot become something by means of something, it necessarily goes on coming forth from that which is without anything; but that which is without anything is for ever without anything. The sage stores away in *it*. (A. C. Graham trans.; his italics)

The sage stores away in that which is forever without anything— which is *no-thing*. How do the myriad things come forth? According to the *Zhuangzi*:

> The knowledge of the ancients was perfect. How perfect? At first, they did not know that there were things. This is the most perfect knowledge; nothing can be added. Next, they knew that there were things, but did not yet make distinctions between them. Next they made distinctions among them, but did not yet pass judgements upon them. When judgements were passed, the Tao was destroyed.

The inner chapters of the *Zhuangzi* conclude: "Hold on to all that you have received from Heaven but do not think you have gotten anything. Be empty, that is all."

Although this language is not Buddhist, don't these passages seem to be describing a similar way of experiencing? In fact, what has been said about naming, functions, and desires (intentions)—how they construct the world we normally take for granted—can help us understand the enigmatic first chapter of the *Daodejing*, which is making exactly the same points. Here is my own rendering (with the assistance of other translations):

> The Dao that can be Dao'd is not the constant Dao
> The name that can be named is not a constant name
> Having-no-names is the source of heaven and earth
> Having-names is the mother of the ten thousand things
> Without desire/intention behold the wonder
> With desire/intention behold the forms
> These two things have the same origin
> Although they are different in name
> Their sameness is called the mystery
> From mystery to mystery: the gate of all wonder!

The first line emphasizes that the Dao is indescribable because it is beyond all names, being unstructured by language. The Dao cannot be Dao'd because that would give it a name, make it into a thing. It is constant, unchanging, because without names or forms that could change. The second line refers to a different way of experiencing that involves naming. The things we name are not constant because they "come and go."

> Having-no-names is the source of heaven and earth
> Having-names is the mother of the ten thousand things

That which has no name, which we nonetheless refer to as the Dao, is the source of everything that manifests. Naming (language) gives birth to all things: our everyday world is constructed by identifying and differentiating things.

Without desire/intention behold the wonder
With desire/intention behold the forms

These two lines point to the hinge between the two ways of experiencing. When there are no desires or intentions (the Chinese term
yu can be translated either way), the world is not objectified into a
collection of utensils, and we can perceive the ineffable mystery that
is the Dao. When we have desires/intentions, we grasp the world and
experience it in the usual utilitarian way, as composed of a multiplicity of (named) forms.

These two things have the same origin
Although they are different in name

Having distinguished these two modes of experience, these lines
now point to their nonduality. They are not two different realities but
two sides of the same reality, reminding us of Nagarjuna's claim that
there is no real difference between samsara and nirvana.

Their sameness is called the mystery
From mystery to mystery: the gate of all wonder!

The final two lines marvel that the world has these two very different aspects and yet is one, like the two faces of a coin. It is a mystery—
but perhaps that mystery becomes a little more comprehensible when
we understand how language preconsciously constructs the world
and how meditation ("mind-fasting" in Daoism) can deconstruct it.

To sum up, our normal preoccupation with trying to satisfy desires
involves grasping the world as a collection of things whose names are
functions; that makes them into utensils for obtaining what we want.
We often need to do that, of course, but when that's the only way we
relate to the world, we overlook something essential: that all the forms
named and grasped—including ourselves—are manifestations of
something in itself nameless, formless, ungraspable, and mysterious.

THE ECOLOGY OF PROPERTY

What does all this imply about our collective relationship with the earth? Daoist emphasis on returning to a more natural way of being part of the natural world inevitably raises the issue of the relationship between human civilization and the biosphere that supports it. Today, of course, that relationship is more strained than it was in the times of Laozi and the Buddha. Two hundred years ago little more than 3 percent of the world's population lived in cities; today well over half of us live in urban areas. According to ecopsychologists, many urbanites suffer not only from various types of overcrowding and pollution but also from what they term "nature deficit syndrome."

Urban environments involve a more utilitarian relationship with one's surroundings, which has important implications for how tightly we are entrenched in the "consensus reality" that experiences the world as a collection of objects for us to use. In cities almost everything we relate to is a utensil, including most people, whom we learn to see in terms of their functions: the shop clerk, the restaurant waiter, the bus driver, and so forth. We live among machines and things produced by machines, whereas in a forest we are embedded in a world where the things we encounter are alive. [In other words, urban areas are constructed in such a way that almost everything and everyone is a *means* for obtaining or achieving something. Surrounded by so many other people busy doing the same thing, it is difficult to *see through* or *let go* of this way of relating to the world and realize that there is another way to perceive it.]

Thinking about utensils raises questions about technology—our larger utensils, in effect. Technologies extend our human faculties, including the ability to instrumentalize the natural world more effectively. According to Michael Zimmerman, "The same dualism that reduces things to objects for consciousness is at work in the humanism that reduces nature to raw material for mankind." Jacques Ellul describes modern technology as "the defining force of a new social order in which efficiency is no longer an option but a necessity imposed on all human activity." Efficiency is not about determining the goals or ends to be valued and sought; it is only about assessing means—in relation to the natural world, measuring how economically we can utilize the world's "resources" (which include us, of course). Is this another example of means swallowing ends?

Max Frisch said that technology is "the knack of so arranging the world that we don't have to experience it. Is modern civilization the knack of so arranging the earth that we don't have to experience it? Of arranging how we live together so we don't notice that we are part of the natural world?

Why don't we notice that? One of the pillars of the worldview we collectively take for granted today is a principle that the ecological crisis exposes as problematic, even dangerous. It is a social construct that, like money, is essential and, like money, has developed in ways that need to be revaluated and reconstructed.

The basic problem with *property*—particularly land—is that, in belonging to someone else (or something else, such as a corporation), it is reduced to a means for the ends of the owner. Despite being indispensable to civilization as we know it, our modern concept of private property is not something natural to human society in the way that, for example, language and material tools are. Hunting and gathering societies that do not grow their food have a very different relationship to the land they live on and the other creatures they live with. This has sometimes led to fateful misunderstandings. When Native Americans "sold" Manhattan to the Dutch for the equivalent of sixty guilders, it is unlikely that both sides to that transaction understood it in the same way. In the end, what mattered is that the Dutch and their successors had the ability to enforce their legal understanding of the agreement. The fact that all conceptions of property are culturally and historically conditioned reminds us that property is not inherently sacrosanct. Our social agreements about property can be changed, and today need to be changed, as part of our response to burgeoning social and ecological crises.

In his *Second Treatise,* the English political philosopher John Locke argued that governments are instituted to secure peoples' rights to "life, liberty, and property," which Thomas Jefferson famously changed to "life, liberty, and the pursuit of happiness" when he wrote the Declaration of Independence. Although in Genesis, God gives the world to all humanity in common, Locke claimed that individual property rights are natural rights. What is less known, however, is the proviso Locke added: that one may appropriate property in this way only if "there is enough, and as good, left in common for others."

In his *Discourse on Inequality*, Jean-Jacques Rousseau, the French Enlightenment philosopher, disagreed with Locke: property is not an inalienable right but a social construct that founded the social order. "The first man, having enclosed a piece of ground, to whom it occurred to say this is mine, and found people sufficiently simple to believe him, was the true founder of civil society." Despite declaring that this hypothetical person was "an imposter" responsible for miseries and horrors, Rousseau nonetheless believed in the importance of that construct: "the right of property is the most sacred of all rights of citizenship."

Although the two views of property are different, they share something more important. Both perspectives are concerned only about the rights of the owner and have nothing to say about the rights of the owned—because property, of course, has none. A more nondualist Buddhist approach, however, suggests a different perspective.

According to the Pali Canon, the Buddha did not challenge the idea of private property. When merchants asked him for advice, he emphasized how one gains wealth and how one should use it. Accumulating wealth for its own sake was condemned, in favor of generosity—which may have something to do with the fact that the monastic community was dependent on lay support. The Lion's Roar Sutta tells a story about a kingdom that collapses when the ruler does not give property to those who are impoverished. The moral is not that poverty-induced crime should be punished severely or that poor people are responsible for their own poverty and should work harder, but that the state has a responsibility to help people provide for their basic needs.

Of course, there was also another side to the Buddha's teachings, [which emphasized nonattachment to material goods and promoted the value of having fewer wants.] Monastics, for example, should be content with the four requisites enough food to alleviate hunger and maintain health, enough clothes to be modest and protect the body, enough shelter to focus on mental cultivation, and enough medical care to cure and prevent basic illnesses. Personal possessions were limited to three robes, a begging bowl, a razor, a needle, a water strainer, and a cord around the waist.

This de-emphasis on personal property is consistent with Buddhist teachings about the self. The word *property* derives from the Latin *proprius*, "one's own." There is no property—whether territory or movable possessions—unless there is someone to own it. The concept is inherently dualistic: the owner objectifies, in effect, that which is owned. Then what does property mean for a tradition that is devoted to realizing there can be no real owner, because there is no self?

In terms of conventional "consensus reality," however, property is obviously a necessary social construct. Why? That brings us back to the basic Buddhist concern: alleviating dukkha—"suffering" in the broadest sense. From a Buddhist perspective, property is a useful social construct insofar as it reduces dukkha but problematic when it increases dukkha. Needless to say, such a perspective is quite different from the prevalent view that largely determines how our civilization relates to the earth today.

So the issue isn't whether I have exclusive access to my toothbrush or similar personal items. The question is whether wealthy people and corporations should be free to own as much property as they want, and whether they should be able to utilize that property (especially land) in any way they want—including ways that damage the earth. Today the bottom line, with few exceptions, is "hands off" if they earned their money legally and bought the property legally. It's theirs, so they can do more or less whatever they want with it. If the earth is to survive the onslaught of our species, however, this social agreement about property needs to be rethought. Instead of focusing only on what is beneficial to one species, what about the well-being of the planet? Is there another alternative besides relating to "it" (we're talking about Mother Earth here!) as something for humans to exploit?

That is not an appeal for socialism, insofar as that means the state owns everything, in effect, on behalf of all its citizens. From an ecological perspective, that usually amounts to a collective version of the same owner-owned, subject–object dualism.

I'm talking about a new freedom movement.

The Next Liberation Movement?

The development of Western civilization has often been understood in terms of greater freedom. According to the historian Lord Acton, the growth of freedom has been the central theme of history. Since the Renaissance there has been progressive emphasis on religious freedom (the Reformation), then political freedom (starting with the English, American, and French revolutions), economic freedom (class struggle), colonial freedom (independence movements), racial freedom (anti-slavery campaigns and civil rights movements), and more recently gender and sexual freedom (women's rights, gay and transgender rights, and so forth).

There is, however, another way to describe this historical development. Almost all of those freedom movements can be understood as struggles to overcome hierarchical exploitation, which are forms of (here it is again!) the means-ends duality. Slavery, for example, has been called "social death" because the life of a slave is completely subordinated to the interests of the master. Patriarchy subordinated women to men in much the same way, exploiting them for domestic work, sexual pleasure, and producing children. Rulers and the people they oppress, colonialists and the colonized, robber barons and workers: they are all versions of inequitable relationships, which were rationalized as natural and therefore proper. In all these cases, freedom means not being a means to someone else's ends. Democracy entails, in principle, that no one's personhood is defined by their subservience to what someone else wants them to do.

What is the next step in this historical progression? Well, what means–ends subordination remains the greatest problem today, now that our extraordinary technological powers have transformed the earth and all its creatures into a collection of resources to be extracted and consumed in whatever ways we humans decide?

If this instrumentalist view of the natural world is at the heart of our ecological predicament, perhaps the next development in overcoming hierarchical means/ends relationships is to appreciate that the planet and its magnificent web of life are much more than just a resource for the benefit of one species. Instead of dismissing such a possibility as an unlikely collective self-sacrifice, this freedom movement can be based on the opposite realization: that the ecological crisis demonstrates our own well-being can't really be distinguished from the well-being of the whole.

According to the "ecotheologian" Thomas Berry, the universe is not a collection of objects but a community of subjects. Our own biosphere is a resplendent example of that community. Humans are not the ultimate end, the goal of the evolutionary process, because no species is—or, better, because every species is. Today we need to think seriously about what it would mean to live on the earth in such a way.

Of course, given entrenched economic and political realities, any social movement in that direction would be an idealistic fantasy.

Except that it's already happening.

"I AM THE RIVER AND THE RIVER IS ME"

Our attitude toward animals has changed considerably from the days when passengers would shoot bison from train windows, just for the fun of it. Today we have animal sanctuaries and laws that protect them from wanton cruelty—and now more radical developments have begun.

According to traditional jurisprudence, nature is property without any legal rights, so environmental laws have focused only on regulating exploitation. Recently, however, the inherent rights of the natural world have been recognized in Ecuador, New Zealand, and India, meaning that cases can be brought up *on its behalf.*

In accordance with the traditional worldview of Quechua peoples in the Andes, Ecuador in 2008 passed a new constitution mandating that the natural world has the right to exist, maintain, and regenerate, making it the first country to legally enshrine the rights of nature. According to its Article 71: "Nature, or *Pachamama*, where life is created and reproduced, has the right for its existence to be integrally respected as well as the right of the maintenance and regeneration of its vital cycles, structures, functions and evolutionary processes. Every person, community, people or nationality can demand from the public authority that these rights of nature are fulfilled."

In New Zealand, what used to be the Te Urewera National Park on the North Island was granted personhood in 2014. The government has given up formal ownership, and the land is now a legal entity with "all the rights, powers, duties and liabilities of a legal person," according to the Te Urewera Act. Among other things, personhood means that lawsuits to protect the land can be brought on behalf of the land itself, without the need to show harm to any human.

This unusual designation is the result of agreements between New Zealand's government and Maori groups, which argued for years over guardianship of the country's natural features. According to Chris Finlayson, New Zealand's attorney general, the issue was resolved by appreciating the Maori perspective. "In their worldview, 'I am the river and the river is me.' . . . Their geographic region is part and parcel of who they are." Pita Sharples, minister of Maori affairs when the law was passed, said that the agreement "is a profound alternative to the human presumption of sovereignty over the natural world." Jacinta Ruru of the University of Otago called the new law "undoubtedly legally revolutionary" not only in New Zealand but for the world as a whole. In 2017 the Whanganui River, the third longest in New Zealand, was also granted personhood.

Also in 2017, a high court in the northern state of Uttarakhand in India declared the Ganges and Yamuna rivers to be legal persons. Later it extended this designation to their tributaries, including glaciers, rivers, streams, rivulets, lakes, air, meadows, dales, jungles, forests wetlands, grasslands, springs, and waterfalls. Citing the new status of the Whanganui River in New Zealand, the judges ruled that the two rivers and their tributaries are "legal and living entities having the status of a living person with all corresponding rights, duties and liabilities."

The Indian ruling is distinctive in two ways. First, that the judges referred to the new status of the Whanganui River in New Zealand as precedent is itself an important precedent that may lead to more such rulings in India and elsewhere. Is the designation of personhood for natural systems such as rivers an idea whose time has come?

Second, unlike in New Zealand, the Indian ruling was in direct response to increasing pollution of the Ganges and Yamuna, and the inability of the federal and state governments to work together to protect the two rivers, which are considered sacred by most Hindus. This precedent is also important. If present legal regimes of property rights are not working to protect threatened ecosystems, it is acknowledged that new ways of thinking and acting may be necessary. (However, the high court judgment was later overruled by the Supreme Court of India as being unenforceable.)

The most radical of these developments, potentially, is Ecuador's new constitution, which does not identify particular areas for special status but enshrines the rights of nature in the whole country. There is an interesting contrast to be made here with the U.S. National Park system, which has been called "America's best idea" by Ken Burns (among others). As Curtis White points out in *We, Robots*, "the National Park system is also our *worst* idea because it puts a boundary on nature beyond which we are free to be as destructive as we like. Drive back across a park boundary and suddenly you're in Petroleum World ('our national automobile slum,' as James Howard Kunstler put it)." The ecological crisis exposes the limits of this dualistic way of thinking. White goes on to say:

> In the age of climate change, the boundary between nature and civilization means nothing. The pine bark beetle that presently ravages forests ever farther to the north was not consulted about these boundaries. ("You can't eat that forest,

it's a National Park!") And that's just a small part of the devastation that will be brought by global warming.

As I write this chapter, there is a "rights of nature" lawsuit seeking personhood for the Colorado River. "There's a growing understanding that environmental frameworks that exist today under environmental laws are not adequate to protect the environment," according to Mari Margil of the Community Environmental Legal Defense Fund, which is acting as legal advisor in the case. "They begin from the wrong place, the wrong premise[that nature is treated as right-less, as property, and therefore we can't even protect its basic right to exist let alone to flourish."]

Granting personhood to some special places will not by itself save us or the earth's biosphere, but it points to an incipient change in our collective understanding of our relationship with the earth. Wendell Berry's poem "How to Be a Poet" says that "there are no unsacred places[There are only sacred places and desecrated places." We desecrate the natural world when we relate to it only as an instrumental means to some other goal (such as economic growth). We re-sacralize it when we realize and respect its own buddha-nature.]

"For every thing that lives is Holy." (William Blake)

We are here to awaken from the illusion of our separateness.

—THICH NHAT HANH

Are God and Mother Nature married, or just good friends?

—RICHARD LOUV'S SON MATTHEW, AGE FIVE

We did not come into this world. We came out of it, like buds out of branches and butterflies out of cocoons. We are a natural product of this earth, and if we turn out to be intelligent beings, then it can only be because we are fruits of an intelligent earth, which is nourished in turn by an intelligent system of energy.

—LYALL WATSON

Our challenge is to create a new language, even a new sense of what it is to be human. It is to transcend not only national limitations, but even our species isolation, to enter into the larger community of living species. This brings about a completely new sense of reality and value.

—THOMAS BERRY

The mind that searches for contact with the Milky Way is the very mind of the Milky Way galaxy in search of its own depths.

—BRIAN SWIMME AND THOMAS BERRY

The earth expounds Dharma, living beings expound it, throughout the three times everything expounds it.

—AVATAMSAKA SUTRA

Heaven is my father and earth is my mother and even such a small creature as I finds an intimate place in its midst. That which extends through the universe, I regard as my body, and that which directs the universe, I regard as my nature. All people are my brothers and sisters, and all things are my companions.

—ZHANG ZAI

If we continue abusing the Earth this way, there is no doubt that our civilization will be destroyed. This turnaround takes enlightenment, awakening. The Buddha attained individual awakening. Now we need a collective enlightenment to stop this course of destruction. Civilization is going to end if we continue to drown in the competition for power, fame, sex, and profit.

   —THICH NHAT HANH

What has become of that opportunity to become more fully human that the "control of nature" was to provide?

   —JOSEPH WOOD KRUTCH

We cannot foresee the future, but we can augur that we are approaching an ethical parting of the ways that will be as decisive as the biological parting, twenty or twenty-five million years ago, between the way that has led to Man and the way that has led to the hominoid apes. Once again, the alternatives may be polar extremes.

   —ARNOLD TOYNBEE

He who loves the whole world as if it were his own body
Can be entrusted with the world.

   —DAODEJING

4

Is It the Same Problem?

TRADITIONAL BUDDHIST TEACHINGS offer us a path to resolve our personal predicament—"us" in this case referring to individuals who have the potential to awaken, one by one. The collective implications of those teachings received little attention and probably could not have been much developed, given their political and historical context. Although the monastic sangha has sometimes been described as the first democracy in human history, no Asian Buddhist society had a democratic polity until the modern era. Many rulers were eager to declare themselves bodhisattvas or even buddhas, but I don't know of any who encouraged Buddhist teachers to examine what might be called the *institutional dukkha* caused by hierarchical and exploitative social systems. Today we really have no choice, given the societal and ecological challenges that confront us, and fortunately our democracies, although defective in ever more obvious ways, still provide enough freedom of religion and freedom of speech for us to do so.

The two previous chapters focus on the individual path of awakening and personal transformation. Chapter 2 unpacks Trungpa's airplane analogy: "Enlightenment is like falling out of an airplane. The bad news is that there is no parachute. The good news is that there is no ground." The airplane is the world as we normally understand it, a "consensus reality" that can be deconstructed and reconstructed[Enlightenment is always an accident, but meditation makes us accident-prone.]When we let go of ourselves, we can realize a groundless ground where there is no security or insecurity because there's no self that needs to be secured.

Chapter 3 says more about why we experience the world in the way we normally do, and how to undo it. Language does not just label the things we perceive; it identifies them by their functions and organizes them into a collection of utensils. This way of constructing the world is not something that "I" do. Rather, the act of grasping creates both the grasper and the grasped, the sense of a self *inside* that feels separate from the objectified world *outside*. In doing so, we constantly overlook that the forms we grasp by naming—including ourselves—are the "presencing" of a generative no-thing-ness that is nameless, formless, and wondrous.

In describing our usual predicament and the Buddhist response, the previous chapters have also drawn out some of the ecological implications. Since awakening involves realizing that we are not separate from each other or from the earth, it becomes apparent that the ways we live together and relate to the earth need to be reconstructed as well. That means collective engagement with *social dukkha*: working together to challenge the problematic economic and political structures that are deeply implicated in the environmental crisis and the social justice issues that confront us today. In experiencing our day-to-day human world mainly as a collection of utensils, we have objectified the natural world into a collection of resources to be exploited. The eco-crisis raises a question that has become inescapable: Do we own the earth, or does the earth own us? Moreover: Do we need to reevaluate the concept of ownership?

This chapter will weave together those various threads to offer a more systematic overview of the relationship between traditional Buddhist teachings and our ecological situation today. That involves something more than just explicating old texts. I haven't been able to find any reference to climate change in the Pali suttas or Mahayana sutras—although, to be honest, I haven't tried very hard. Gautama Buddha lived in a very different time and place, Iron Age India about 2,400 years ago. His life and teachings suggest deep appreciation of

the natural world, yet say nothing about global warming, ozo
or species extinction events—which shouldn't surprise us, si
of them was a problem in his day. It's worth noting that, like his con-
temporaries, he also knew nothing about carbon dioxide or any element of the periodic table, nor the cellular structure of life, DNA, or
innumerable other scientific facts we take for granted now. That's not
a criticism, of course, but a reminder Buddhism is not only what the
Buddha taught but what the Buddha began—and we keep the tradition alive by keeping it relevant to our situation.

So what does Buddhism have to offer us now, as we struggle to
respond to an unprecedented ecological emergency? As the previous
chapters have emphasized, what the Buddha did know about was
dukkha, "suffering" in the broadest sense: not only pain but dissatisfaction, discomfort, anxiety . . . Basically, the reality of dukkha means
that it is the nature of our unawakened minds to be bothered about
something. Gautama declared that what he taught was dukkha and
how to end it, which does not mean that life is always miserable but
that even those who are wealthy and healthy normally experience a
dis-ease that keeps gnawing away inside.

What can that contribute to our understanding of the ecological
crisis? Our rapidly deteriorating situation certainly causes dukkha—
an enormous amount, both human and nonhuman!—but how is that
collective dukkha related to the individual dukkha that the Buddha
focused on? This chapter explores what seem to me precise and
profound parallels between our perennial personal predicament,
according to traditional Buddhist teachings, and the contemporary
predicament of our now-global civilization. Like many others, I have
argued that the eco-crisis is as much a spiritual challenge as a technological and economic one; unpacking those similarities will help to
flesh out that claim.

Does this mean that there is also a parallel between the two solutions, individual and collective? Does the Buddhist response to our
personal predicament also point the way to resolving our collective
one? We shall see.

The Individual Predicament

Our usual individual predicament, which is fundamentally the same now as it was in the Buddha's day, can be summarized as follows:

1. The self is a psychological and social construct.
2. That construct involves a sense of separation from the world "outside," which causes anxiety.
3. That anxiety (*lack*) includes confusion about who I am and the meaning of my life.
4. In response, I try to ground myself in ways that often worsen my situation.
5. I cannot get rid of the self but can realize that it is "empty."
6. This realization frees and empowers me to help "others."

The first claim, that the self is a psychological and social construct, is a truism of developmental psychology. To be fully human is more than a biological achievement: babies are not born with a sense of self. Socialization is essential. A mother (for example) looks into her baby's eyes and says its name. The baby not only learns to identify with that name, it eventually learns to see itself in the way that mother sees it—as a self, a special type of thing inside that is separate from and quite different from the other things outside.

Where Buddhism differs from most of modern psychology is its implicit claim that there is something inherently uncomfortable about this construct. In addition to physical and mental pain, and the dissatisfaction often caused by impermanence (especially when I contemplate my own), a self that feels separate from the rest of the world *is* dukkha.

Classical psychoanalysis, and much psychotherapy still, is preoccupied with identifying and resolving trauma due to painful events that happened earlier in one's life. "If only that hadn't happened, I wouldn't be so unhappy today . . ." From a Buddhist perspective, however, the internalization of a sense of self, although necessary in order to function in the world, is nonetheless problematic in itself. As previous chapters have explained, the basic problem isn't what happened, it's that "I" happened. Since the *sense* of self is a construct, it does not correspond to anything substantial. It's not a real thing but a bunch of interactive functions: perceiving, feeling, acting, reacting, remembering, planning, intending . . . which means it is normally anxious and insecure, because there's nothing there that could be secured. In other words, it is ungrounded and ungroundable, which reminds us of Trungpa's airplane analogy. It's not that the self inside the airplane is grounded and loses that grounding when it falls out. Inside the plane the self experiences its ungroundedness as a *lack*: the sense that, even when things are going well, there is something wrong with me. Falling out of the airplane and experiencing my groundlessness are simply realizing my true nature—what has always been the case.

This is the core of the ignorance that Buddhism emphasizes. We try to secure ourselves by identifying with things "outside" us that (we think) can provide the grounding we crave: money, material possessions, reputation, power, physical attractiveness, and so forth. David Foster Wallace calls these the things we worship. I have offered other terms for these obsessions: "lack projects" (because we believe they will fill up our sense of lack) or "reality projects" (because we believe they will make us feel more *real*). We normally misunderstand our dis-ease as due to lack of such things. Since none of them can actually ground or secure one's sense of self, it means that no matter how much money, fame, and so on, we may accumulate, it never seems to be enough.

Tragically, many of those efforts to solve the problem involve manipulating other people in ways that reinforce the actual problem—the sense that there is a "me" that's separate from others. Trying to secure myself by grasping something ends up objectifying and devaluing the world into a means for my never-quite-achieved ends: the place where my lack projects happen. Any other value or meaning that the world may have tends to be ignored in the process.

The Buddhist solution to this predicament is not to "get rid of" the self. That cannot be done and does not need to be done, inasmuch as there never was a separate self to be gotten rid of. It is the *sense* of self that needs to be deconstructed (e.g., "forgotten" in meditation) and reconstructed (e.g., replacing the "three poisons" of greed, ill will, and delusion with generosity, loving-kindness, and the wisdom that recognizes our interdependence). In keeping with the etymological meaning of *Buddha* as "an awakened one," Buddhism is literally "WakeUp-ism"—because its path involves seeing through the illusion of separation. I am not inside, peering out at an objective world outside. Instead, "I" let go of lack-project attempts to ground myself and realize my groundlessness in a mysterious world where everything else is also groundless, manifesting something—better, a *no-thing*—that is ungraspable and unknowable but is constantly presencing in manifold forms.

Lack projects involve self-preoccupation: the meaning of my life is about *me*. Realizing my groundlessness liberates me from that self-centeredness and transforms the world as well, because it's no longer just the place where I play my lack-project games. That also changes the meaning of my life. Although I'm free now to live as I like, that will naturally be in a way that contributes to the well-being of the whole, because I don't feel separate from that whole. The focus shifts from "how can I become more *real?*" to "what can I do to make this a better world for all of us?"

Amazingly, this Buddhist account of our individual predicament corresponds quite precisely to our ecological situation today.

OUR COLLECTIVE PREDICAMENT

We not only have individual senses of self, we also have group selves. I'm not only David Loy; I am male, a white person, a U.S. citizen, and so forth. And just as one's individual sense of a separate self tends to become problematic, so collective senses of self are often problematical, because they too distinguish the *inside* from the *outside*: men from women, white from black, Americans from Chinese, and so forth. Those of us who are inside are not only different from those outside; we like to think that we are better than them, but in any case the sense of separation rationalizes pursuing our own well-being at their cost. Obviously, a lot of the world's problems occur because of such group selves, big and small.

The issue here is whether "separate self = dukkha" also holds true for our largest collective sense of self: the duality between us as a species, *Homo sapiens sapiens*, and the rest of the biosphere. In fact, there are remarkable parallels between the individual sense of self and humanity's collective sense of self:

1. Like the personal sense of self, human civilization is a construct.
2. This construct too has led to a collective sense of separation (alienation) from the natural world, which causes dukkha.
3. This dukkha involves anxiety, including uncertainty about the meaning and direction of our now-global civilization.
4. Our main response to that alienation and anxiety—the collective attempt to secure or "self-ground" ourselves—is making things worse.
5. We cannot "return to nature," but we can realize our nonduality with the rest of the biosphere, and what that implies.
6. This collective realization will clarify what it means to be human. Being a species that is part of something greater than ourselves, our role is to serve the well-being of that whole—which will also heal us.

Let's unpack these parallels.

Chapter 2 discussed Loyal Rue's claim that Axial Age religions such as Christianity and Buddhism encourage indifference to social and ecological issues, because they emphasize cosmological dualism and individual salvation. In a famous essay on "The Historical Roots of Our Ecologic Crisis," Lynn White Jr. traced our contemporary alienation from the natural world back to Christian arrogance toward nature, based on such anthropocentric texts as Genesis 1:28: "Fill the earth and subdue it, and have dominion over the fish of the sea and over the birds of the air and over every living thing." Hugh Brody in

The Other Side of Eden focuses on this "farmer's version of history" as the pivotal moment in our dislocation from the natural world. For hunter-gatherers, in contrast to agriculturalists, "everything is founded on the conviction that home is already Eden and that exile must be avoided." We are reminded of Lame Deer's cooking pot, its relationship with the clouds, sky, and four-legged creatures.

Even if we think of ourselves as post-Christian, our now global civilization still takes for granted "the Christian axiom that nature has no reason for existence save to serve man. . . . Despite Darwin, we are *not*, in our hearts, part of the natural process. We are superior to nature, contemptuous of it, willing to use it for our slightest whim" (Lynn White Jr.). For traditional Christianity, the earth becomes merely a backdrop for the human drama of sin and salvation.

Western civilization is usually understood to have two roots: Judeo-Christianity and classical Greece. Greece was another Axial Age culture, although its form of cosmological dualism was humanistic rather than religious. The thinkers of classical Greece reinforced the Judeo-Christian gulf by discovering a hitherto-unappreciated difference between human society and the natural world: our social structure—how we live together—is a collective construct that we can reconstruct.

The claim that human civilization is a construct seems so obvious that it's difficult for us to understand an alternative view. Today we take for granted that there are many ways to live together. If the democratic process of passing new laws isn't working well, reform movements and revolutions are possible. Nevertheless, this self-evident claim was not evident to archaic societies. The modern world owes that insight to Greece, which around the Buddha's time began to distinguish *nomos*—the conventions of human society (including culture, technology, and so on)—from *physis*, the natural patterns of the physical world. The Greeks realized that, unlike the natural world, the social conventions that constitute society can be reconstructed. Plato, for example, offered detailed plans to restructure the Greek city-state in two of his dialogues, the *Republic* and the *Laws*. Today, of course, we are familiar with many such models, but when we study his *Republic*, we are reading something that was quite revolutionary in its time.

The important point is that archaic civilizations in Mesopotamia, Egypt, India, and China accepted their own traditional and hierarchical social structures as inevitable, because they were assumed to be just as natural—and therefore just as sacred—as their local ecosystems. The same was true of the Maya, Incas, and Aztecs of the New World, which is especially interesting because, although those three cultures influenced each other a little, there was no known influence from any of the Eurasian empires. This agreement suggests that, as more complex civilizations developed, it was *natural* for them to think of their own social structures as natural. Does that mean our modern distinction between nature and human society, inherited from the Greeks, is *unnatural* in some way?

In those civilizations, rulers were sometimes overthrown, but new rulers invariably replaced them at the apex of the social pyramid, which was also a religious pyramid. Kings were gods or godlike in that they played a unique role in communicating with the deities that supervised our created world. This highlights something else that such societies did not develop but we today take for granted: the distinction between political power (the state) and religious authority (the church). To play one's part in society and to be religious—to serve the gods—amounted to the same thing. One supported the hierarchical social order, which was sacred, and thereby the rituals of the god-king and his priests.

The most significant difference between such civilizations and ours today—and this brings us to the main point—is that all of them believed they had an important role in keeping the cosmos functioning harmoniously, and if they didn't perform that task, then the universe would break down or fall apart. Probably the best-known example is the Aztecs, who performed mass human sacrifice because blood was needed to keep the sun god on his course through the heavens. The Sumerians in Mesopotamia believed that humans have been created by the gods to be their servants, and if we didn't serve them (by offering sacrifices, for example), the gods would be displeased—and you don't want to upset the gods!

In Hinduism the term *dharma* not only meant cosmic law, which created the universe from chaos, but also designated human behavior, both ethical and ritualistic, which maintained the cosmic as well as the social order. Different castes had different *dharmas*, which is why it was important to uphold the caste system.

In short, distinctions we now take for granted between the natural world, the social order, and religion did not exist for these ancient civilizations.

Understanding one's own society as natural was used to justify social arrangements unacceptable today, of course. None of the civilizations mentioned above was democratic or had an independent legal system to defend one's human rights. Nevertheless, there was a positive side. Believing that the structure of their society was part of the natural order, and that humans had an important role to play in keeping that natural order harmonious, conferred an extraordinary psychological benefit. The members of such cultures shared, and took for granted, a sense of *meaning* that we today no longer have—indeed, that we can hardly conceive of. Because they understood their society to be built into the cosmos, their social function was also built into the cosmos. Both personally and collectively, they knew why they were here and what they had to do.

Today, however, the meaning of our individual lives and our societies has become something that we have to decide for ourselves in a universe whose meaningfulness (if it has any) is not something we agree on. Religion for most of us in the modern world has become a matter of personal preference, a freedom we celebrate, but the fact that we are so aware of other options diminishes the psychological security that exclusive affiliation traditionally provides. While we enjoy many freedoms that archaic societies did not provide and would not freely give them up, the psychological price of those freedoms is that we have lost the basic comfort that comes from "knowing" one's role in society and the role of one's society in the cosmos.

The upshot of all this—for better and worse—is increasing anxiety about who we are and what it means to be human. Loss of faith in the life orientation provided by traditional religion has left many of us rudderless. Our ever more powerful technologies enable us to accomplish almost anything we want to do, yet we don't know what we *should* do. Insofar as we can no longer rely on God or godlike rulers to tell us, we are thrown back upon ourselves, and the lack of any grounding in something greater than ourselves has become a profound source of dukkha, collective as well as individual.

Our situation today is well expressed in the concluding sentences of Yuval Harari's book *Sapiens: A Brief History of Humankind*:

> Despite the astonishing things that humans are capable of doing, we remain unsure of our goals and we seem to be as discontented as ever. We have advanced from canoes to galleys to steamships to space shuttles—but nobody knows where we're going. We are more powerful than ever before, but have very little idea what to do with all that power. Worse still, humans seem to be more irresponsible than ever. Self-made gods with only the laws of physics to keep us company, we are accountable to no one. We are consequently wreaking havoc on our fellow animals and on the surrounding ecosystem, seeking little more than our own comfort and amusement, yet never finding satisfaction.
>
> Is there anything more dangerous than dissatisfied and irresponsible gods who don't know what they want?

The heart of the problem—*why* we don't know what we want—is that we no longer believe we have any role to play in the cosmos. Since we "know" that humans, like all other species that have evolved, are mere accidents of genetic mutation, we are accountable to no one and no thing beyond ourselves. All we can do, then, is enjoy ourselves—if we can, while we can, as long as we can—until we die.

No wonder we feel dissatisfied and act irresponsibly.

To sum up, today our sense of separation from the natural world has become an ongoing source of alienation and frustration. This explains parallels one through three, above: modern human civilization as our collective construct involves individual uncertainty about what it means to be human and collective uncertainty about where our now-global civilization is going and what it should be doing.

That brings us to point number four. What has been our collective response to this predicament?

To highlight the parallel with our individual situation, let's remember how we usually respond personally. Our individual predicament is that the sense of a separate self is shadowed by a sense of *lack*: the feeling that something is wrong with me. Normally we misunderstand the source of the problem and project it outward. What's wrong with me is that *I don't have enough* of something: money, consumer goods, prestige, and so on. Since these are only symptoms of the true problem, I can never obtain enough of them to allay the sense of *lack* at my core. In fact, my efforts to do so may actually aggravate the situation. Attempts to manipulate others tend to reinforce the sense of separation between us. . . . Is there a collective version of all this?

I believe there is. It hinges on our obsession with "progress," a slippery term. That word derives from the Latin *pro-gressus*, "to advance or walk forward." But surely progress is a good thing? The problem is that the term has been hijacked to validate the consequences of continuous economic growth and never-ending technological development, whatever the social and ecological costs. The implication is that, although there may be some adverse "byproducts" to such developments, they can be fixed—usually by more of the same economic and technological growth, which will provide us with more resources to solve such problems.

Nevertheless, we may wonder: When will we consume enough? When will corporate profits and stock prices and our collective gross national product be large enough? When will we have all the technology we need? These questions seem odd because we know there are no limits to those ever-escalating processes, but isn't there something odd about *that?* Why is *more and more* always *better* if it can never be *enough?* If progress means walking forward, how do we know we are headed in the right direction? Are we trying to go somewhere, or are we trying to get away from something?

We are back in the now-familiar issue of means and ends. It's another version of the problem with power—which is a good servant but a poor master. Technological and economic growth in themselves may be valuable *means*, insofar as they can provide the resources to accomplish what we want to do. They are not good as ends-in-themselves, because they cannot answer the basic human question about what it means to be human and what we should be doing with all those resources. Since, however, we have no other answer to that basic question—none that we collectively agree on, anyway—technological and economic development have become, in effect, a substitute. The means have become the ends. They function as forms of secular salvation that we seek but never quite attain. Not knowing where to go or what to value, our civilization has become obsessed with ever-increasing power and control.

What do we seek? Modern civilization is built on the estrangement between nature and culture. We no longer feel grounded in the natural world, which creates the burden of trying to create our own ground—*self-grounding* ourselves, in effect. And what we are discovering, ecologically as well as psychologically, is that it can't be achieved technologically. We are becoming more anxious and compulsive, not less. We are haunted by a collective sense of *lack.*

Chapter 3 pointed out that, in perceiving the world as a collection of utensils, we tend to instrumentalize the present. My sense of *lack* drives me to focus on the future, when (I hope) it will finally be resolved, as I achieve my goals; then I will be satisfied and content. Our collective focus on "progress" amounts to the same thing. The promise of technological and economic development is that the world will be better in the future if we utilize the present as the means to get there. Instead of getting better, however, the changes happening in the present continue to accelerate and become more and more stressful. The future continues to beckon, but for some reason we never get there.

This way of understanding our collective situation suggests that the ecological crisis is unavoidable. Any techno-economic system that needs to keep growing (to stave off collapse) will sooner or later bump up against the limits of the biosphere. But there are different ways to understand what the basic problem is. From the perspective of those committed to that system, the solution is more of the same: more technological development (more efficient solar panels, for instance) and more economic growth (more jobs in the solar- and wind-power industries). Although both may be important, this characteristic reliance on a technological salvation is also a symptom of the larger challenge, insofar as increasing dependence on sophisticated, ever more powerful technologies tends to aggravate our sense of separation from the natural world. If the parallels discussed in this chapter are valid, any successful solution to the larger problem—modern civilization's collective sense of separation and alienation from the natural world—must involve recognizing that we are an integral part of the earth.

So does that solution involve "returning to nature"? Remember the individual parallel: I can't get rid of the self because it never existed. Nor do I want to get rid of my sense of self, which is necessary to function in the world. Rather, I need to realize that the self is "empty," an impermanent manifestation of something greater, which I do not grasp but open up to.

In a similar fashion, we cannot return to the natural world because we have never left it.

Look around yourself. Even if you're inside a windowless room, everything you see, whether human-made or not, is derived from nature: wood from trees, plastic from oil, metal from ores, concrete from cement and sand and gravel . . . and let's not forget to include our own bodies and clothes. The environment is not only an "environment"— that is, not just the place where we happen to be located. Rather, the biosphere is the ground from which and within which we arise. We are not in nature, we *are* nature. The earth is not only our home, it is our mother. Before we make it into a resource, it is The Source.

In fact, our relationship with Mother Earth is even more intimate, because we can never cut the umbilical cord. Fantasies about terra-forming Mars reveal less about the potential of an extraterrestrial colony than how estranged we have become from our planetary home. Our bodies don't end at our fingertips and toenails. The air in your lungs, like the water and food that enter your mouth and pass through your digestive system, is part of a greater holistic system that circulates through each of us. Human bodies are made of the same elements that compose the oceans, rivers, mountains, and trees. Our blood is salty because it duplicates our original ocean home. We share at least 98 percent of our DNA with chimpanzees and bonobos. Buddhadasa Bhikkhu reminds us what this means:

> The entire cosmos is a cooperative. The sun, the moon, and the stars live together as a cooperative. The same is true for humans and animals, trees and the earth. Our bodily parts function as a cooperative. When we realize that the world is a mutual, interdependent, cooperative enterprise, that human beings are all mutual friends in the process of birth, old age, suffering, and death, then we can build a noble, even a heavenly environment. If our lives are not based on this truth then we'll all perish.

Our species has never been separate, just (as Thomas Berry puts it) "autistic."

A COLLECTIVE ENLIGHTENMENT?

To understand intellectually that I am part of something greater than myself is different from *real*-izing that in a transformative experience. And when we consider the collective parallel, the challenge becomes much greater. How could the conceptual understanding presented above resolve the basic anxiety that haunts our global civilization now, when we must create our own meaning in a world where God has died? Archaic worldviews and the "taken for granted" meaning of life they provided are no longer a serious option. But what other alternatives are possible for us?

Highlighting this parallel means asking what collective transformation might correspond to the individual awakening that Buddhism traditionally promotes. "The Buddha attained individual awakening. Now we need a collective enlightenment to stop the course of destruction" (Thich Nhat Hanh). This chapter concludes with some reflections on what that might mean.

One of the mysterious aspects of Buddhist awakening is that, if there is no self, who or what is it that awakens? The "new cosmology" proposed by Thomas Berry and Brian Swimme offers an answer: humans are a way that "the universe reflects on and celebrates itself in a special mode of conscious awareness." Or, more simply, "we are the self-consciousness of the universe." Our species is how the universe becomes self-conscious. If we understand biological evolution as the way our self-organizing cosmos has become not only more complex but more conscious, that suggests a different perspective on the nature of our self-consciousness.

The question is, what is the *self* that has become self-conscious? We humans can pat ourselves on the back in celebration of our special mode of awareness, yet from a Buddhist perspective our consciousness is usually flawed by the delusion that it is the consciousness of an individual self that is separate from other selves and the rest of the world. The Buddhist path (like other nondualist spiritual traditions) emphasizes the importance of realizing that we embody something greater: that consciousness is not something an individual self has, but that the sense of self is one of the ways that consciousness manifests.

In other words, to say that we are the self-consciousness *of* the universe means that the self that's conscious is the universe itself. When Mara questioned the Buddha's enlightenment—"Who testifies that your awakening is genuine?"—what did the Buddha do? He said nothing but simply touched the earth. To cite my favorite Buddhist quotation, which Dogen used to describe his own awakening: "I came to realize clearly that mind is nothing other than rivers and mountains and the great wide earth, the sun and the moon and the stars." The implication is that biological evolution needs to be supplemented by this type of spiritual and cultural evolution, which takes the next step to reveal our nonduality with Mother Earth. It turns out that our true self is also our true home.

This way of understanding Buddhist-type enlightenment—as the next step in human evolution—also gives us a different perspective on the ecological crisis. Of course our collective sense of separation from the earth has led to trashing the planet. How could it not, when the earth is valued only as means to satisfy our self-centered goals? The eco-crisis is a spiritual challenge as much as a technological and economic one because it prompts us to take that next step. Thich Nhat Hanh's claim that we need a collective enlightenment to stop the course of destruction points to the fact that we now need to evolve spiritually in order to survive physically.

If so, it becomes all the more urgent to clarify what *collective enlightenment* means. If awakened beings such as Gautama Buddha are prototypes for the larger cultural transformation that's necessary, does collective enlightenment mean that a significant percentage of individuals awaken in the traditional Buddhist sense, or something else? It's difficult to imagine what that "something else" might be. It's even more difficult, however, to believe that an enormous number of practitioners will awaken soon enough to form a group savvy enough to lead the kind of social movement necessary to resolve our ecological predicament quickly enough.

Or is the problem here that this understanding of enlightenment is too narrow? We might be looking in the wrong place, thus missing what we are looking for—a social revolution in consciousness and engagement that may already be happening.

A relevant point here is that Buddhist traditions have conceptualized individual enlightenment in different ways. Within East Asian Buddhism historically one of the main debates has been about whether awakening is sudden or gradual. Although "forgetting oneself" and letting go as discussed in chapter 2 can lead to an abrupt experience of groundlessness, that's not the only way profound transformation can happen. Despite his own famous experience of sudden enlightenment, Dogen emphasized that zazen (Zen meditation) is not a means to that goal, for zazen itself manifests the unattached and formless true nature of our minds. To do *shikan taza* ("just sitting") in that spirit is also to let go and be changed, even if we are not aware of it at the time. It's been compared to walking through a meadow early in the morning. We may not notice for a while that our clothes have become damp from the dew on the grasses.

What would a collective version of gradual enlightenment be like? That more specific question is easier to answer, because it may already be happening.

In his book *Blessed Unrest: How the Largest Movement in the World Came into Being, and Why No One Saw It Coming*, Paul Hawken documents the emergence of a worldwide network of socially engaged organizations that has arisen in response to the global challenges that threaten us today, social justice issues as well as ecological ones. This "movement of movements" is both the largest ever—at least two million organizations, maybe many more—and the fastest growing. "It's the first time in history that a movement of such scale and breadth has arisen from within every country, city, and culture in the world, with no leader, rulebook, or central headquarters. . . . It is vast and the issues broadly defined as social justice and the environment are not separate issues at all."

In an interview published in *Tricycle* magazine, Hawken traces the origins of this movement all the way back to the sacredness of life and compassion espoused by various Axial Age religions, but it has no common ideology:

> Bear in mind that ideology is what has gotten humanity into trouble every time and it won't serve us here. Every 'ism' ends up in schisms, including Buddhism, and in the case of most 'isms'

the results are violence, war, and cruelty. The gift of this movement is that it is already atomized. It is not an ism, it cannot divide. It can only come together. It is something we've never seen before in human history. Consequently, we have no name for it.

Most striking of all is the metaphor that Hawken uses to describe this movement. It is the "immune response" of humanity, arising as if spontaneously to protect us and the planet from the forces that are despoiling our world. The organizations that compose this movement are "social antibodies attaching themselves to the pathologies of power." He devotes a whole chapter to unpacking this analogy.

> Just as the immune system recognizes self and non-self, the movement recognizes what is humane and what is not humane. Just as the immune system is the line of internal defense that allows an organism to persist over time, sustainability is a strategy for humanity to continue to exist over time. The word *immunity* comes from the Latin *im munis,* meaning ready to serve.

Note that an immune system is part of something greater than itself, which it serves by defending. White blood cells do not have a problem figuring out what their role is. Given the kinds of infections that confront our collective immune system today, this parallel too seems obvious. We are here to help the earth to heal—a process that will also heal us. This may be a new way of understanding the Buddhist path but this path is not new, as Hawken points out:

> In terms of commitment, I think Buddhist practice is by its very nature social change. It cultivates compassion, which is the source of transformation. The word means to "suffer with" or "suffer together." Thus compassion arises from a deep place of receptivity and listening that is the beginning of healing. What we are talking about broadly is the healing of the world, a journey of a thousand years.

A Zen practitioner, he sees Buddhism as a growing part of this movement:

> Buddhism as an institution will become much more engaged in social issues, because I cannot see a future where conditions do not worsen for all of us. The gift of the years ahead is that we cannot address the salient issues of our time and be the same people we are today. *Dukkha*, suffering, has always been the crucible of transformation for those who practice.

Buddhism is not about avoiding suffering but being transformed by it—which suggests there's lots of transformation in our future.

Because Hawken focuses on social engagement, he does not emphasize that this also seems to be the beginning of a fundamental transformation in human consciousness. "Today millions of citizens work on behalf of people they will never know or meet, and it is astonishing that altruism guides and permeates the fastest growing movement in the world." Joanna Macy makes the same point:

> Wherever I go with workshops, I find the readiness to experience a collective awakening. I'm astonished by how explicit this is. It's a sense of wanting to belong to the Earth, aching for reverence for the Earth. Again and again, I believe that people would be ready to die for our world, to save the life process. There is something pressing within the heart-mind that is just huge. It's happening very fast.

So is the collective enlightenment that Thich Nhat Hanh calls for already happening? As a small part of this worldwide movement, might Buddhism play a distinctive role in encouraging not only the liberation of consciousness but the application of liberated consciousness to the social and ecological crises that challenge us today?

Nonetheless, we should remember (as Hawken does) that immune systems sometimes fail, and "this movement most certainly could fail as well." Pathogens such as the human immunodeficiency virus (HIV), which causes AIDS, kill their host by destroying the body's immune system. Is there another, less hopeful parallel here with the earth's immune system? It remains to be seen how resilient the biosphere's ecosystems are, and how successful its collective immune response will be.

If current trends continue, we will not.

—DANIEL MAGUIRE

If we don't win very quickly on climate change, then we will never win. That's the core truth about global warming.

—BILL MCKIBBEN

We're under some gross misconception that we're a good species, going somewhere important, and that at the last minute we'll correct our errors and God will smile on us. It's delusion.

—FARLEY MOWATT

The apocalypse is not something which is coming. The apocalypse has arrived in major portions of the planet and it's only because we live within a bubble of incredible privilege and social insulation that we still have the luxury of anticipating the apocalypse.

—TERENCE MCKENNA

That civilizations fall, sooner or later, is as much a law of history as gravity is a law of physics.

—PAUL KINGSNORTH

The end of the human race will be that it will eventually die of civilization.

—RALPH WALDO EMERSON

Civilization is a disease almost invariably fatal unless the cause is checked in time.

—DEAN INGE

We are acting as if we had a colossal death wish.

—JOANNA MACY

If we want to learn to live in the Anthropocene, we must first learn how to die.

　　—Roy Scranton

It is possible that intelligence in the wrong kind of species was fore-ordained to be a fatal combination for the biosphere. Perhaps a law of evolution is that intelligence usually extinguishes itself.

　　—E. O. Wilson

Humanity will get the fate it deserves.

　　—Albert Einstein

You can hold back from the suffering of the world . . . but per-haps this very holding back is the one suffering you could have avoided.

　　—Franz Kafka

Ought we not, from time to time, open ourselves to cosmic sadness?

　　—Etty Hillesum

Grief is the price we pay for love.

　　—Elizabeth II

The task is to move from happy endings to mature serenity in a world without happy endings.

　　—Paul Shepard

Despair is the suicide of imagination. Whatever reality presses upon us, there still remains the possibility of imagining something better, and in this dream remains the frontier of our humanity and its possibilities. To despair is to voluntarily close a door that has not yet shut.

　　—Sam Smith

It's too late to be a pessimist.

 —ANONYMOUS

When doomsday comes, if someone has a palm shoot in his hand, he should plant it.

 —MUHAMMAD

5

What If It's Too Late?

Too late for what?

When I wonder about our ecological future, the cautionary examples of Easter Island and St. Matthew Island often come to mind.

The story of Easter Island is well known, largely due to its *moai*, monumental stone statues. It is one of the remotest inhabited places on earth, over a thousand miles from its nearest populated neighbor, Pitcairn Island. When Dutch ships first encountered the island on Easter Sunday 1722, they discovered a society of two to three thousand people, barely surviving in a deforested ecosystem with few natural resources. Archaeologists have determined that Polynesians originally arrived between 700 and 1100 AD, and that their population eventually grew to about 15,000 people. At that time there were twenty-one species of trees and many land birds, all of which eventually went extinct. When the native tropical forest was cut down, the topsoil it protected eroded and agriculture sharply declined. The loss of trees also meant inability to construct fishing boats, and middens show that around that time the diet switched from fish and dolphin protein to seabirds. Soon the vast colonies of seabirds also collapsed, leaving domesticated chickens as the main source of protein. Artistic figures from this period show distended bellies and exposed ribs. Many of the islanders moved into fortified caves with evidence of warfare and perhaps cannibalism.

The overexploitation of Easter Island's natural resources led to ecological disaster, yet humans survived, although in much reduced circumstances. The story of St. Matthew Island is quite different, but just as disturbing.

St. Matthew is a remote island in the Bering Sea, off the coast of Alaska. During World War II the United States Coast Guard set up a small base to monitor radio communications, and in 1944 introduced twenty-nine reindeer as an emergency food source, which turned out not to be needed. When the base was abandoned a few years later, the reindeer were left, and by 1963 their population had multiplied to about six thousand. During the next two years, however, their numbers collapsed, due to limited food supply and an exceptionally cold winter. A few years later only forty-two reindeer remained, and by the 1980s they had died out.

Something similar happened to rabbits introduced to tiny Lisianski Island west of Hawaii in the early 1900s. Without any predators, they reproduced and ate themselves to death within a decade. None survived.

The exhaustion of natural resources on Easter Island was more gradual than the collapse of the food supply on St. Matthew and Lisianski Islands, and humans are of course much more adaptable than deer or rabbits. But I think it would be unwise to depend too much on our ingenuity, in the face of the unprecedented ecological problems we have created for ourselves. To revisit a few of the statistics mentioned in chapter 1: in my lifetime, global population has more than trebled, from about 2.5 billion people in 1947 to 7.7 billion in early 2018. Over a third of the earth's arable land has been lost over the last forty years, and the UN's Food and Agriculture Organization predicts that the world has just sixty more years of growing crops with the industrial agricultural practices presently used.

Given those challenges, and our obvious inability to respond adequately—so far, anyway—we cannot evade the question that most of us would rather not think about. What if it has become too late to avoid civilizational collapse—or worse? James Lovelock, who first proposed the Gaia hypothesis, warned in 2009 that the world's population might sink as low as 500 million over the next century due to global warming. He also claimed that attempts to tackle climate change will not be able to solve the problem but merely buy us time.

Many other scientists are predicting an "apocalyptic" future—a term used by James Hansen, formerly head of NASA's Goddard Institute for Space Studies and perhaps the world's most famous climate researcher. He believes that catastrophic climate change is inevitable unless we completely de-carbonize our energy sources by 2030. Researchers at the University of Hawaii predict "historically unprecedented" climates perhaps as soon as 2047. In his 2010 book *Eaarth: Making a Life on a Tough New Planet*, Bill McKibben, one of the founders of 350.org, emphasizes that we are well past the point of no return. Thinking "we need to do something for our grandchildren" is out of touch with reality, for we're already living on a planet from a parallel universe (hence "eaarth"):

> The Arctic ice cap is melting, the great glacier above Greenland is thinning, both with disconcerting and unexpected speed. The oceans are distinctly more acid and their level is rising . . . The greatest storms on our planet, hurricanes and cyclones, have become more powerful . . . The great rain forest of the Amazon is drying on its margins . . . The great boreal forest of North America is dying in a matter of years . . . [This] new planet looks more or less like our own but clearly isn't . . . This is the biggest thing that's ever happened.

Paleontologists variously estimate that 95–98 percent of all the species that have ever lived on earth have disappeared, most of them in dramatic and relatively sudden extinction events. We are now well into the planet's sixth extinction event, in this case caused by one particular species—us—and it is quite possible that we will become one of the victims. Fred Guterl in *The Fate of the Species* and Clive Hamilton in *Requiem for a Species* both argue that human extinction is a very real danger, because, as the Stanford biologist Paul Ehrlich bluntly puts it, "In pushing other species to extinction, humanity is busy sawing off the limb on which it perches."

Until recently most scientists have been reluctant to make such claims but more are becoming vocal about the very real possibility of human disappearance. For example, in a 2010 interview with the *Australian* newspaper, Frank Fenner, a distinguished emeritus professor of microbiology at Australian National University, predicted that the human race will probably become extinct within the next hundred years, due to population explosion and unrestrained consumption. "It's an irreversible situation. I think it's too late. . . . Mitigation would slow things down a bit, but there are too many people here already."

Fenner is not a climate scientist, so can we ignore what he thinks? Is the danger of human extinction a fantasy to scare us into greater efforts at remediation? What is more of a fantasy is the widespread belief that the kind of industrial growth economy promoted by the government of every "advanced" nation can continue indefinitely without wrecking the biosphere.

Global warming is already causing many problems, but the bottom line for our species is that our physical bodies simply cannot endure the higher temperatures that are becoming likely. In a 2013 essay Bill McKibben pointed out the danger of persistent "wet bulb" conditions exceeding 35°C and with very high humidity:

> At such temperatures, for reasons of physiology and physics, humans cannot survive . . . it is physically impossible for the environment to carry away the 100W of metabolic heat that a human body generates when it is at rest. Thus even a person lying quietly naked in hurricane force winds would be unable to survive.

In sustained wet bulb conditions our bodies cannot cool themselves by perspiring but instead absorb heat from the air, resulting in hyperthermia. After six hours they begin to break down. Climate scientists agree that much of the earth becomes uninhabitable if average global temperatures go up by 4°C (7.2°F). For Steven Sherwood, a meteorologist at the University of New South Wales, Australia, that would be "catastrophic," and in most of the tropics life would become "difficult, if not impossible." Four degrees Celsius may not seem like a lot because we are used to more extreme variations during the twenty-four hours of a day, but even a 2–3°C average increase would mean temperatures regularly surpassing 40°C (104°F) in North America and Europe, and much higher temperatures nearer the equator. "The warmest July in the Mediterranean region could be nine degrees Celsius [16.2°F] warmer than today's warmest July" (George Marshall). At such temperatures complete wet bulb conditions are not necessary for our bodies to break down, which is how the 2003 heat wave in Europe could kill over 70,000 people. Unfortunately, it is becoming increasingly unlikely that we will be able to avoid that 2–3°C average increase.

One reason why this is so difficult for us to appreciate is that over the last 10,000 years or so—during which civilization, including agriculture, developed—both carbon dioxide levels and the earth's climate have been remarkably constant. We therefore take this stability for granted, but "for most of the last 100,000 years, an abruptly changing climate was the rule, not the exception," according to the paleontologist Peter Ward. "We have no experience of such a world." His book *Under a Green Sky: Global Warming, the Mass Extinctions of the Past, and What They Can Tell Us about Our Future* provides evidence that all previous global extinction events (except perhaps for the disappearance of dinosaurs sixty-five million years ago) happened because of rapid global warming due to increased atmospheric carbon dioxide levels. Slow climate change gives species time to adapt by evolving; rapid warming does not.

But just how rapid is "rapid"? Until recently scientists believed that during the most recent extinction event, the Paleocene-Eocene Thermal Maximum (PETM) about fifty-five million years ago, global temperatures increased by 5–8°C over about 20,000 years, but new sediment data indicates that it actually happened "in the geologic blink of an eye." According to a 2013 paper in the Proceedings of the National Academy of Sciences, after a sudden big increase in atmospheric carbon the ocean surface turned acidic within a few weeks or months and *global temperatures rose by 5°C within about thirteen years.*

What climactic disturbance could suddenly cause something like that? The danger that threatens us is not only sustained emissions of carbon dioxide but "tipping points" that may be close or have already passed, in which a positive feedback loop occurs. A well-known example is the albedo effect. Arctic snow and ice reflect most of the solar radiation they receive, whereas the ocean surface absorbs most of it. Due to higher temperatures, more Arctic and Antarctic ice melts, which exposes more surface water, which absorbs more heat, which causes more ice to melt—and so on.

Although I'm not a scientist, climate or otherwise, what I've read suggests that the most ominous tipping point is the danger of a "methane burp." Methane is a carbon compound gas seventy-two times more potent than carbon dioxide over a twenty-year period. It is the principal component of the natural gas burned to heat homes, ovens, water heaters, and so on. Since the year 1750 methane in the atmosphere has increased about 150 percent, to a level that is now over twice as high as anytime in the previous 400,000 years. There are many sources of atmospheric methane, including agriculture, farm animals, and leakage during hydraulic fracturing ("fracking"), but by far the greatest quantities of methane are presently trapped in permafrost and under ocean floor sediments, both of which are rapidly warming today. Alan Weisman, in *The World without Us*, estimates that 400 billion tons of methane are buried in permafrost alone. Daniel Rirdan's book *The Blueprint: Averting Global Collapse* claims that if all that permafrost methane were released, it would be equivalent to ten *trillion* tons of carbon dioxide. In comparison, the current amount of all greenhouse gases released into the atmosphere is equivalent to about forty-four *billion* tons of carbon dioxide each year.

Without a scientific background, I'm not in a position to evaluate these numbers. In comparison to all the talk of carbon dioxide emissions, we don't hear much about the threat of methane discharges. But scientists themselves seem to be increasingly concerned. The release of large amounts of methane has been suggested as a possible cause of at least two extinction events, the Permian–Triassic and the Paleocene–Eocene Thermal Maximum. Will history repeat itself?

WAITING FOR THE APOCALYPSE

The original Greek word *apocalypse*, often translated as "revelation," more literally means "unveiling." It involves the disclosure of some hidden or obscured knowledge, "a vision of heavenly secrets that can make sense of earthly realities" (Bart Ehrman). As commonly understood, however, the term refers to what will happen in the "last days," when many people believe that the world will experience a dramatic and climactic transformation. The best-known example is in the Book of Revelation, the last book of the Bible, which recounts what Jesus purportedly divulged to John of Patmos regarding the approaching end times.

Yet there is another way to understand *apocalypse:* as a forthcoming revelation about the nature of human civilization and the radical changes that must occur, one way or another. In that sense perhaps some sort of apocalypse has become unavoidable.

Not all religions prophesy an apocalypse, but they are found in both Abrahamic and non-Abrahamic traditions, including Buddhism. These usually include a messiah or avatar, who will appear to assist or ameliorate the process, often by struggling against evil forces.

The Abrahamic traditions believe in a linear cosmology, in which the world attains final and permanent redemption. In Judaism the last days include the end of the Jewish diaspora, appearance of the messiah, and resurrection of the righteous into a sanctified world. Some Christian sects anticipate a time of tribulation—sometimes a thousand years—before Christ returns to defeat the Antichrist and inaugurate the Kingdom of God. Muslims await the Mahdi redeemer who will reign over the world for some years and then, with the help of Isa (Jesus), usher in the Day of Resurrection and Judgment.

Non-Abrahamic traditions, including Hinduism and Buddhism,

usually have more cyclic worldviews, with long periods of deterioration followed by restoration of a golden age, and then the whole cycle recurring. For Hinduism, Kalki, the final incarnation of Vishnu, will appear on a white horse to end the present Kali Yuga. According to the Pali Canon and later Buddhist texts, Gautama Buddha predicted that his teachings—the true Dharma—would decline for many hundreds of years, during a period of physical decay and moral degeneration, until the next Buddha Metteya (Maitreya) would appear to revive the Dharma. This belief influenced the way some Buddhist traditions developed. For example, Pure Land Buddhism in East Asia emphasized devotional practices to attain the Pure Land because, in this degenerate age, enlightenment is otherwise too difficult to attain.

Most Buddhist adherents in Asia are familiar with Maitreya, the Buddha to come, although there is no agreement about when he is likely to appear. Today, however, belief in any messiah or avatar—who will arise to save us from ourselves or from the mess we have made of things—is more difficult to credit. Thich Nhat Hanh has said that the next Buddha might appear as a sangha, as a community of practitioners. Must we collectively become the one we have been waiting for?

Much less known than prophecies about Maitreya is a more catastrophic prediction in the Anguttara Nikaya of the Pali Canon, where Gautama Buddha describes the ultimate fate of our world: a series of seven suns will dry out the earth and then burn it up:

> There will come a season, O monks, when after hundreds of thousands of years, rains will cease. All seedlings, all vegetation, all plants, grasses and trees will dry up and cease to be.

A second sun will evaporate all brooks and ponds. The third sun will dry up rivers, the fourth lakes, and the fifth oceans. The sixth sun "will bake the earth even as a pot is baked by a potter." When the seventh and final sun appears, "the earth will blaze with fire until it becomes one mass of flame. . . . So impermanent are conditioned phenomena, so unstable, so unreliable."

It is unclear how literally we should take this story, which concludes by encouraging practitioners not to be attached to this world.

The description of each sun ends with the same admonition: "It is enough to become disenchanted with all conditioned phenomena, enough to become dispassionate toward them, enough to be liberated from them."

The Anguttara text is also unclear about whether this destruction is only part of a larger *kalpa* cycle. In any case, what is striking is how similar this account is to scientific predictions about the eventual fate of our planet. When the sun runs out of hydrogen in another seven billion years or so, it will become a red giant that swallows Mercury, Venus, and probably the earth. However, long before that—probably within the next billion years—increasing radiation from the sun will boil and then bake our planet, leaving no atmosphere, no water, and surface temperatures of hundreds of degrees. No life of any kind will be possible.

There are different ways to respond to this grim reminder of our ultimate fate. We can refuse to accept this extermination of humanity and all other life forms. So much has been achieved technologically over the past few hundred years; what might we accomplish over the next hundred thousand? Already self-funded visionaries like Elon Musk are planning to establish Martian colonies . . . but how would any life on Mars survive the death of our sun? And even if it becomes possible to colonize other solar systems, their suns too will eventually suffer the same fate. What we now know about the nature of the universe implies that, sooner or later, our extinction is inevitable.

That destiny encourages us to reflect on what this scenario means for our usual future-oriented ways of thinking and acting. Why does the eventual but inevitable annihilation of human life make us uneasy today? Given the more immediate problems that confront us, a billion years certainly seems like nothing to worry about, but if all life as we know it will come to an end, sooner or later, what does that imply about how we live *now*?

Evolutionary psychology has conditioned us individually to focus on getting our genes into future generations. Is that the source of our discomfort with any thought of extinction? Yet Buddhist emphasis on impermanence and insubstantiality implies that evolutionary history is not necessarily destiny. What has been conditioned can be deconditioned and reconditioned, which is what the Buddhist path encourages.

The End of Life As We Know It?

What do you do when nothing you do can avail?

—Shin'ichi Hisamatsu

Buddhist teachings remind us to acknowledge the "I don't know" aspect of our predicament, rather than become dogmatic about what will happen in the future—or, for that matter, about what is actually happening right now. There is a fundamental mystery to the universe, including our own lives, that we do not and perhaps cannot understand. Nevertheless, we should not fall back on that mystery to dismiss or ignore scientifically based predictions, in the belief that some god or buddha or good karma or awakening will save us from what we are doing to the world.

So let us contemplate the worst-case scenario that some scientists are publicly or privately predicting: that it is already too late to avoid tipping points (such as a massive release of buried methane), which will cause a rapid and catastrophic increase in surface temperatures. Let's suppose that this increase will bring about not only the collapse of civilization but also human extinction within a hundred years or so. Think of it as a thought experiment, if you like. How might Buddhism help us cope with this collapse?

Preparing for one's own individual death has always been an important part of the Buddhist path, but anticipating the death of our species is something more than a collective version of the same thing. "We all know we are going to die, and we used to be able to cope with the thought that our life was contributing to something larger that would survive us. Now even that has been taken away from us" (Bill McKibben). Most of us wish to leave the world a slightly better place, one way or another. We want our children and grandchildren to be happy. I hope that some people might benefit from this book, but if our species goes extinct, there will be no one to read it. If humanity disappears, Buddhism and all other religious traditions will also disappear, along with the compositions of the greatest musicians, the paintings and sculpture of the greatest artists, the poetry and plays and novels of the greatest writers, the discoveries of the greatest scientists, and so on. Take a moment to reflect on that. . . . How should we live today, in the face of that very real possibility?

A few contemporary teachers have begun to address these concerns, including two of the very best: Thich Nhat Hanh and Joanna Macy.

Thich Nhat Hanh's contribution to *A Buddhist Response to the Climate Emergency* is frank about our situation. "We are like sleepwalkers, not knowing what we are doing or where we are heading. . . . We have to start learning how to live in a way that a future will be possible for our children and grandchildren." Not just for a good future but for *any* future. A 2012 interview published in the online journal the *Ecologist* reflects further on the possible disappearance of our species. Thich Nhat Hanh begins by mentioning the Permian–Triassic extinction some 252 million years ago and then considers its lesson for us today:

> Now a second global warming is taking place. . . . If 6 C degrees take place, another 95 per cent of species will die out, including *Homo sapiens*. That is why we have to learn to touch eternity with our in breath and out breath. Extinction of species has happened several times. Mass extinction has already happened five times and this one is the sixth. According to the Buddhist tradition there is no birth and no death. After extinction things will reappear in other forms, so you have to breathe very deeply in order to acknowledge the fact that we humans may disappear in just 100 years on earth.
>
> You have to learn how to accept that hard fact. You should not be overwhelmed by despair. The solution is to learn how to touch eternity in the present moment. We have been talking about the environment as if it is something different from us, but we are the environment. The non-human elements are

our environment, but we are the environment of non-human elements, so we are one with the environment. We are the earth and the earth has the capacity to restore balance and sometimes many species have to disappear for the balance to be restored. . . . When we are mindful of our body and what is going on around us we are in a situation to touch the miracle of life that is going on around us. This present moment is full of wonders. If you don't know how to touch these wonders you do not know how to appreciate life—to appreciate what is there.

Those familiar with Thich Nhat Hanh's teachings will not be surprised that he emphasizes breathing deeply in order to "touch eternity" right here and now. When we are truly in this present moment, we touch the miracle of life. But his discussion of mass extinction, including our own, adds something else: "According to the Buddhist tradition there is no birth and no death." What does that teaching—already mentioned in chapter 2—mean in light of the possibility of our own physical disappearance?

In a 2011 interview—with the endearing title "It Looks Bleak. Big Deal, It Looks Bleak"—Joanna Macy was asked about her response to the sixth extinction, which may include our own species, and where she derives the psychic resources to bear witness to it:

Yes, it looks bleak. But you are still alive now. You are alive with all the others, in this present moment. And because the truth is speaking in the work, it unlocks the heart. . . . This may be the last gasp of life on Earth, and what a great last gasp, if we realize we have fallen in love with each other. If you are really in the moment of experiencing our reality, you don't say "Oh I won't experience this because it's not going to last forever!" You've got this moment. It's true for now. We can have a reasoned concern about what is down the track, without necessarily getting hooked on something having to endure.

Ecobuddhism: A few climate scientists consider we may have already entered into runaway climate change.

Joanna: I suspect that they are right. Logically they are right: we don't have a snowball's chance in hell. At my last workshop, people were saying "It's too late" in the *Truth Mandala* that we do. And then they went out and got arrested at the White House, chained to the fence to protest the wars. So our acting with passionate dedication to life doesn't seem to be affected. I would just as soon live that way . . . With the little time left, we could wake up more. We could allow this whole experience of the planet, which is intrinsically rewarding, to manifest through our heart-minds—so that the planet may see itself, so that life may see itself. And we can bless it in some way. So there is some source of blessing on us, even as we die. I think of a Korean monk who said "Sunsets are beautiful too, not just sunrises." We can do it beautifully. If we are going to go out, then we can do it with some nobility, generosity and beauty, so we do not fall into shock and fear.

. . . I think there is a drive within living systems to complexify, to wake up—there is an evolutionary movement. I speak out of the love and excitement generated by my little work, which many people are doing with me. It does require being able to experience pain. It does require tears and outrage. It does require *positive disintegration*. Our whole culture needs positive disintegration. It has to die to itself. So my Christian upbringing is relevant there: Good Friday and Easter, the necessity for death and rebirth. We are going to die as a culture, and it's better for us to do it consciously, so we don't inflict it on everyone else.

The two interviews are quite different, because their ways of teaching are quite different, but Thich Nhat Hanh and Joanna Macy agree about more than the seriousness of the ecological crisis. Both emphasize that our bleak situation provides the best incentive to wake up and realize something about the present moment, something that is very important for our response to the unfolding catastrophe. Macy says that truly experiencing the present moment, alive with others, enables us to participate wholeheartedly in the great adventure of our time. Thich Nhat Hanh adds that we must realize what Buddhism teaches—that there is really no such thing as birth or death.

"Touching the present moment" sounds deceptively simple and easy. Thich Nhat Hanh came of age during the Vietnam War, when his experience of widespread suffering and death motivated him to found the School for Youth in Social Services in Saigon, a grassroots relief organization that rebuilt bombed villages, established schools and medical centers, and resettled homeless families. Later he traveled to the United States, where he urged the government to withdraw from Vietnam, and then led the Buddhist delegation to the Paris Peace Talks—in both cases unsuccessfully. After the war ended, the new Vietnamese government would not allow him to return, so he became an exile living mainly in France, where he founded Plum Village.

I mention this background to emphasize that Thich Nhat Hanh is intimately aware of something else that is usually necessary for our transformation: grief.

Grief has been a central theme in Joanna Macy's work. One of her earliest books was titled *Despair and Personal Power in the Nuclear Age,* and for many years she has guided people through a process that she originally described as "despair and empowerment" work. It is grounded in the insight that despair is not only a psychological reaction to individual suffering but an appropriate response to what we are doing to the planet and ourselves. In a 1999 online interview with Mary NurrieStearns, she spoke about the importance of feeling despair fully to enable its transformation into compassionate action:

> We have to honor and own this pain for the world, recognizing it as a natural response to an unprecedented moment in history. We are part of a huge civilization, intricate in its technology and powerful in its institutions, that is destroying the very basis of life. When have people had this experience before in our history? . . .

People fear that if they let despair in, they'll be paralyzed because they are just one person. Paradoxically, by allowing ourselves to feel our pain for the world, we open ourselves up to the web of life, and we realize that we're not alone. I think it's a cardinal mistake to try to act alone. The myth of the rugged individual, riding as the Lone Ranger to save our society, is a sure recipe for going crazy. The response that is appropriate and that this work elicits is to grow a sense of solidarity with others and to elaborate a whole new sense of what our resources are and what our power is.

For Macy, despair and grief are not the final collapse of our aspirations for the world but necessary for those who aspire to follow the path of spiritual engagement. Her 2012 book *Active Hope: How to Face the Mess We're in without Going Crazy* integrates despair into a transformative spiral that starts with *coming from gratitude,* which enables us to *honor our pain for the world,* followed by *seeing with new eyes,* and only then *going forth* to engage in what she calls the Great Turning. Beginning with gratitude—remembering to appreciate the beautiful web of life that we are part of—provides the foundation for the whole process. "Coming from gratitude helps build a context of trust and psychological buoyancy that supports us to face difficult realities in the second phase." Instead of begrudging our fate, we learn to cherish it, as she exclaims in the 2011 interview: "How lucky we are to be alive now—that we can measure up in this way."

Today Macy's seminal insights have become widely acknowledged. Charles Eisenstein begins a 2016 article, "Grief and Carbon Reductionism," by quoting the environmentalist Michael Mielke: "We came back over-and-over to the realization that the climate movement must proceed through the several stages of grief to get to Acceptance." Eisenstein elaborates:

The grief is essential in order to integrate on a deep level the reality of the situation we face. Otherwise it remains, to most people, theoretical. After all, our social infrastructure insulates us pretty well from the tangible effects of climate change (so far). For most people, compared to say their mortgage payment or their teenager's addiction problem, climate change seems quite remote and theoretical—something that is only happening in the future or on the news. As long as that is the case, they will not take meaningful action either, and it won't change through persuasion. . . . As long as grief is not fully experienced, then normal still seems normal. Even if one is intellectually persuaded of the reality and gravity of climate change, the felt reality is still, "It isn't real," or "It's gonna be fine." . . .

[The attitude of instrumental utilitarianism toward nature—that is the problem.] I'm talking about the idea that the world outside ourselves is basically a pile of resources whose value is defined by its utility. If that doesn't change, nothing will change. And for that to change, for us to see nature and the material world as sacred and valuable in its own right, we must connect to the deep part of ourselves that already knows that. [When we make that connection and feel the hurts of the planet, grief is unavoidable.]

I think that what Thich Nhat Hanh experienced, and what both Joanna Macy and Charles Eisenstein also emphasize, is exactly right: despair and grief are not hindrances that interfere with our wholehearted engagement but an essential part of the ecodharma path. It's not enough to accept the scientific evidence (as marshaled in chapter 1 of this book) or understand how language organizes our perceptions in problematic ways (as explained in chapter 3). We must feel more deeply in order to be transformed more deeply—in Zen language, in order to solve the great collective koan of our time: how to respond to the horrific things we are doing to the earth and to ourselves. That means opening up to the repressed grief and despair that so often paralyze us, whereupon they can transform into compassionate action.

How does grief do that? When deeply felt, it can cut through our usual self-preoccupied ways of thinking and feeling and acting. Most of our habits are self-centered, and conceptual understandings by themselves do not challenge our comfortable lifestyles, as Eisenstein points out. Despair and grief can even lead to "letting go" of ourselves—that is, dissolve the constructed sense of separation between ourselves and that which we are grieving for. Then "my" grief becomes the grief of the earth itself, and my concern for its well-being is grounded in something more profound than utilitarian considerations. As John Seed writes:

> When humans investigate and see through their layers of anthropocentric self-cherishing, a most profound change in consciousness begins to take place. Alienation subsides. The human is no longer an outsider, apart. Your humanness is then recognized as being merely the most recent stage of your existence . . . you start to get in touch with yourself as mammal, as vertebrate, as a species only recently emerged from the rain forest. As the fog of amnesia disperses, there is a transformation in your relationship to other species, and in your commitment to them. . . . "I am protecting the rain forest" develops to "I am part of the rain forest protecting myself. I am that part of the rain forest recently emerged into thinking."

Macy's and Eisenstein's insight about the importance of grief and despair also gives us insight into the problem of climate change denial. From that perspective, the underlying reason for such denial isn't "fake news" or inability to understand what's happening. It's that many people don't *want* to understand, because of what that would imply.

Three psychological explanations for climate denial are commonly offered. The first is that we don't have enough information or there is too much disinformation; yet people often reject or resist the information that they are exposed to. A second explanation is cognitive dissonance, in the sense that we can believe something without it affecting what we do; we can be genuinely concerned about the effects of climate change in the future without that influencing our daily lives now, as Eisenstein points out. Although both of those can be factors, the primary issue is the way emotional blockage and social pressure work together to encourage us to repress the problem. The best book I've read on climate change, George Marshall's *Don't Even Think about It: Why Our Brains Are Wired to Ignore Climate Change,* explains why:

> The bottom line is that we do not accept climate change because we wish to avoid the anxiety it generates and the deep changes it requires. In this regard, it is not unlike any other major threat. However, because it carried none of the clear markers that would normally lead our brains to overrule our short-term interests, we actively conspire with each other, and mobilize our own biases to keep it perpetually in the background.

Ironically, the more dangerous the eco-crisis becomes, the more we are motivated to deny it. This seems counterintuitive, but overwhelming someone with facts—trying to scare them into getting involved—is usually counterproductive. Ernest Becker realized how this works: the more we are reminded of our mortality, the deeper we emotionally invest in our social group, the more passionately we defend its worldview and values, because they are "cultural anxiety-buffers" that provide a sense of security. It's similar to religious affiliation. Humans are mimetic animals: we learn what is real, what is important, what to want and what to do, by internalizing the belief system of the tribe we identify with. Emotion (fear) and the need to fortify oneself within the group subordinate reason and facts. Truth is a function of what one's tribe believes; the rest is "fake news." In other words, our attitudes toward the climate crisis are not personally but socially constructed, largely by pressures to conform that make it difficult to ask uncomfortable questions.

Although this is sobering, it also implies its own solution—as George Marshall points out:

> We also have a virtually unlimited capacity to accept things that otherwise might prove to be cognitively challenging once they are supported within a culture of shared conviction, reinforced through social norms, and conveyed in narratives that speak to our "sacred values." . . . People will willingly shoulder a burden—even one that requires short-term sacrifice against uncertain long-term threats—provided they share a common purpose and are rewarded with a greater sense of social belonging.

And our inclination to share such burdens may be very different in a few years, as the natural disasters continue to pile up . . .

No Death and No End to Death

Thich Nhat Hanh's response to the possibility of our own extinction emphasized "touching eternity with our breath" because in that eternity there is no birth and no death. This basic Buddhist teaching, which was discussed in chapter 2, becomes even more important when we contemplate not just our own individual mortality but an extinction event that might end up including our own species. If there's really no death, however, what is there to be concerned about? Without death, does it even make sense to talk about an extinction event? But then why does the Heart Sutra say that there is "no old age and death, and *no end to old age and death*"?

Many religions address our fear of death by postulating a soul that does not perish with the body. The Buddhist denial of a soul or self (the teaching of anatta) does not allow for that kind of immortality. Instead, Buddhist teachings focus on something that, on the face of it, seems to make no sense: *the unborn.* You and I cannot die insofar as we were never born.

Note that such teachings are not making a claim about what happens to us after we die physically. That our true nature is unborn is not another way of asserting that our minds are immortal. Rather, realizing the unborn reveals something about the nature of our experience, and the self that supposedly has such experiences, right here and now.

An important Zen koan, one of Tototsu's three barriers, points to the same insight. "When you have realized your true nature, you can free yourself from life-and-death. How will you free yourself from life-and-death when your eyes are falling to the ground [when you are at the point of death]?" The key to this koan is the realization that life and death are not events that happen *to* me—to some self-existing consciousness that is separate from such processes. Insofar as there is no such self that is born or dies, there is nothing to fear, because there is nothing to gain or lose. The way to escape birth and death, then, is to "forget yourself" in birth and death, to let go of the usual sense of a separate self that is *experiencing* the birthing or dying, and instead completely *become* the birthing and dying. When at the time for dying there is nothing but the process of dying—neither resisting it nor embracing it—then *death too is "empty."*

The Diamond Sutra expresses this paradoxically: when countless beings have been led to nirvana, actually no beings at all have been led to nirvana. Dogen's articulation is unsurpassed and perhaps unsurpassable:

> Just understand that birth and death is itself nirvana. There is nothing such as birth and death to be avoided; there is nothing such as nirvana to be sought. Only when you realize this are you free from birth and death.

Although such traditional Buddhist teachings focus on our individual situation, they also have implications for how we collectively relate to the ecological crisis. It is not only that you and I are unborn, for everything is unborn, including every species that has ever evolved and all the ecosystems of the biosphere. From this perspective, nothing is lost when species (including our own) become extinct, and nothing is gained if our species survives and thrives.

And yet that perspective is not the only perspective. We are reminded of the Heart Sutra's pithy formulation: form is not other than emptiness, emptiness is not other than form. Yes, from the shunyata emptiness side, there is no better or worse, no-*thing* is born or dies, but that does not negate the fact that *emptiness is form*: that what we call emptiness—the unlimited, constantly transforming generativity that can become anything, according to conditions—has taken form as this awesome, incredibly beautiful web of life, which includes us. However, even that way of expressing it is inadequate, because still dualistic in describing the generativity as something separate from the forms "it" assumes. We cannot avoid the paradox: although *form is emptiness* means that nothing really dies in an extinction event, because there is no(separate)thing to die, nonetheless *emptiness is form* means that emptiness *is* nothing other than this inexpressibly magnificent world, which is rightly called sacred because it is to be cherished more than anything else.

There is a Zen koan about this paradox of extinction/no extinction.

THE GREAT KALPA FIRE

In Indian cosmology a *kalpa* (*kappa* in Pali) is a complete world-cycle, usually billions of years, that encompasses the creation, deterioration, destruction, and then re-creation of the universe. The term *kappa* is found in the Pali Canon, and the concept accompanied Buddhism to China, which is how it came to be incorporated into a Chan/Zen koan.

Case 30 of the *Book of Serenity* is Dasui's "Kalpa Fire."

> A monk asked Dasui Fazhen, "When the great kalpa fire bursts out, the whole universe will be destroyed. I wonder if *It* will also be destroyed or not."
>
> Daizui said, "Destroyed."
>
> The monk said, "If so, will *It* be gone with the other [the universe]?"

Daizui said, "Gone with the other."

A monk asked Longji Shaoxiu, "When the great kalpa fire bursts out, the whole universe will be destroyed. I wonder if *It* will also be destroyed or not."

Ryusai said, "Not destroyed."

The monk said, "Why is it not destroyed?"

Ryusai said, "Because it is the same as the whole universe."

This koan is the only one (as far as I know) about the annihilation of our world. That can mean the "seven suns" that the Buddha forecast or scientific predictions about what will happen to the earth when our sun becomes a red giant. In any case, it applies to any extinction event that includes humanity among its victims.

The koan is enigmatic in two ways. Dasui and Longji give opposite answers to the same question. Who is correct? Can they both be right? Even more puzzling is Longji's final response: although the universe will be destroyed, *It* will not be destroyed because . . . it is the same as the universe!

To make sense of all this, we must understand what *It* refers to. My Zen teacher, Yamada Koun, sometimes referred to emptiness as our "essential nature" or even our "true self," but regardless of the term preferred, the important point is that there is no reference here to any cosmological dualism—no nirvana that transcends this world, for example. According to Yamada's commentary on this koan, "We may imagine that there's something that is void and there's also something that has a form, and yet the two are equal with each other. But this is not right. Rather, seen from one side that 'something' is empty, but seen from the other, it has form."

So it is wrong to think that *It* exists separate from universe. It is nothing other than the true nature of all things in the universe. Insofar as emptiness is not other than form, when the billion worlds of the universe perish in the great kalpa fire, *It* too is destroyed, because all forms perish.

From the other perspective, however, all those forms are empty. All things are subject to destruction, but that which has no form cannot be destroyed, even when the whole universe is destroyed. Yamada writes: "How is it not destroyed? *The destruction itself is* It. So both answers are true."

In trying to describe shunyata, it is almost impossible to avoid falling into the dualism that the Heart Sutra warns us against. Language pushes me into making *no-thing*-ness into a *something* that I characterize in one way or another. But the relationship between form and emptiness cannot be understood in terms of subject and predicate. Just as the universe is not some*thing* that is evolving but is the "empty" evolutionary process itself, so destruction is not something that dualistically happens *to* the universe but another "empty" process. That is why the destruction too is nothing other than *It*.

The spiritual path is living that paradox: it is destroyed, it is not destroyed—the two sides of one coin, back and palm of the same hand. Within that paradox, questions about too late or not too late lose their sting. We do not deny or ignore the possibility of civilizational collapse or even human extinction. Although we don't know what will happen, we are not paralyzed by those possibilities. In the end, too late or not doesn't make any difference to what we are called to do right now.

What does that mean for our engagement with our endangered world: what we do in response to the eco-crisis, and how we do it?

Mindfulness must be engaged. Once there is seeing, there must be acting. Otherwise, what is the use of seeing?

—Thich Nhat Hanh

Because the relationship between self and world is reciprocal, it is not a matter of first getting enlightened or saved and then acting. As we work to heal the Earth, the Earth heals us. No need to wait. As we care enough to take risks, we loosen the grip of ego and begin to come home to our true nature.

—Joanna Macy

In Buddhist practice we say congratulations because now is the time we have been practicing for. No more just practicing the dance. We must now dance. And this is not a dress rehearsal.

—Zenju Earthlyn Manuel

When I am asked if I am pessimistic or optimistic about the future, my answer is always the same: if you look at the science about what is happening on earth and aren't pessimistic, you don't understand the data. But if you meet the people who are working to restore this earth and the lives of the poor, and you aren't optimistic, you haven't got a pulse.

—Martin Keogh

If we want to know what to do, we need to ask the people who pay the highest price for the economic and ecological violence that pervades the earth—and these would be children, women, people of color, and the localized poor. They don't need guidelines, they need rights and honor.

—Paul Hawken

Nobody made a greater mistake than he who did nothing because he could do only a little.

—EDMUND BURKE

They say my work is just a drop in the ocean. I say the ocean is made up of drops.

—MOTHER TERESA

If you are on a boat that is going straight towards a big waterfall, it's of no use to play soft music.

—MATTHIEU RICARD

To know there is a choice is to have to make the choice.

—URSULA LE GUIN

When we are the most in need of compassion, what is the greatest compassion that God can bestow on us? He makes us compassionate.

—IBN 'ARABI

I propose assaulting ourselves and others with compassion. I recommend heavy doses of creativity and courage. I advise doing something well beyond the cultural current of the main stream. At this point, what have you got to lose? Indeed, what have *we* got to lose?

—GUY MCPHERSON

QUESTION: What can I do as an individual?
BILL MCKIBBEN: Stop being an individual.

We don't have the right to ask whether we will succeed. We must just do the right thing.

—WENDELL BERRY

A friend of mine once attended a City Council meeting in her local community and ran into a woman who was repeatedly raising the issue of banning plastic bags. Discouraged, the woman said that she could not seem to earn the respect of the City Council. My friend replied: "You don't need respect. You need a friend. One person is a nut. Two people are a wake-up call. Three people are a movement."

—LAMA WILLA MILLER

We must rebel not as a last act of desperation but as a first act of creation.

—SAM SMITH

Action is the antidote to despair.

—EDWARD ABBEY

The grounds for hope are in the shadows, in the people who are inventing the world while no one looks, who themselves don't know yet whether they will have any effect, in the people you have not yet heard of.

—REBECCA SOLNIT

You are not Atlas carrying the world on your shoulder. It is good to remember that the planet is carrying you.

—VANDANA SHIVA

6

What Shall We Do?

BUDDHIST TEACHINGS do not tell us *what* to do in response to the ecological crisis, but they have a lot to say about *how* to do it.

Gautama Buddha lived about 2,400 years ago in what is now northeast India. Over the next millennium Buddhism spread to most of Asia, interacting with local cultures, assuming a variety of forms. None of those Buddhisms was modern, or global, or confronted an ecological catastrophe that threatened civilizational collapse and perhaps even human extinction. The Buddha said that what he taught was dukkha and how to end it, but the dukkha caused by an eco-crisis was never addressed—because the issue never came up.

This means that humanity's greatest challenge ever is also Buddhism's greatest challenge ever. Previous chapters have explored how Buddhist teachings can help us understand our situation today, but, given its history, it is not surprising that Buddhism can't advise us on what specifically to do about it. In fact, perhaps the biggest danger for Buddhism today is the conviction that premodern versions of Buddhist teaching and practice remain sufficient, especially the belief that the path is all about pursuing our own personal liberation from this mess. Fortunately, Buddhist emphasis on impermanence and insubstantiality encourages a more creative response. Our concern to bring Buddhist principles to bear on the collective types of dukkha that challenge us today is how we remain true to the tradition today.

According to a "Dharma Teachers Collaborative Statement about Climate Disruption" drafted by thirty Dharma teachers around the world, three kinds of action are required: personal, communal, and systemic. Personally, we must curb our consumerism and become more frugal in use of resources, including energy. Collectively, we need to dialogue with friends, neighbors, and our broader communities on the gravity of our situation, which can lead to coordinated action. This is especially relevant to Buddhist organizations. Of the three jewels, it seems to me that Western Buddhists have a lot of Buddha (teachers) and Dharma (teachings), but are often deficient in Sangha (communities). At Dharma centers we listen to talks by teachers and perhaps meet one-on-one briefly with the teacher, but otherwise focus tends to be on group meditation in silence, with maybe a little informal conversation over tea at the end. That's not enough to develop the kind of community bonds that will be even more essential in the future. When more difficult times come, the most important thing will not be whatever food we may have stored in the basement, but whether we are a part of a loving community whose members are prepared to be there for each other. Western Buddhism hasn't focused on this because we still understand the path as the individual pursuit of individual awakening—which fits nicely, of course, into the individualism of modern Western culture, especially in the United States.

The third kind of action the Collaborative Statement calls for is structural: we must work toward more sustainable alternatives to the institutions that are responsible for the policies devastating the earth.

> Above all we must replace profligate political, social, and economic systems with new paradigms more conducive to human flourishing and to harmony between humanity and the earth. In this we should not be afraid to engage politically, thinking we will thereby be "tainting" our spiritual practice. If change is going to occur at all, we have to stand up against the powerful fossil fuel interests that infiltrate the halls of power; we have to put pressure on our elected representatives to follow the call of moral integrity and the trail of science, not the call of the CEOs and the trail of dogma.

Although Buddhist teachings do not say much about evil per se, the "three poisons" (or three fires) of greed, ill will, and delusion are sometimes described as the three roots of evil. When what I do is motivated by any or all of them (and the three tend to reinforce each other, of course), my actions are unwholesome and tend to result in suffering. That is an important insight about how our individual motivations and intentions function, but it has broader implications, because the three poisons also function collectively. Today we not only have much more powerful technologies than in the Buddha's time, we also have more powerful institutions, which operate according to their own logic and motivations—in effect, *they take on a life of their own*. Buddhist emphasis on motivation therefore provides a distinctive perspective on some of our most important social problems and social structures. The ecological crisis continues to worsen because our present economic system institutionalizes greed, our militarism institutionalizes ill will, and the corporate media institutionalize the political and consumerist delusions that support the other two.

The challenge is enormous; there is so much to do. What should we focus on?

The members of our local ecodharma group in Boulder, Colorado, are engaged in a variety of responses. When my partner and I bought a new home, one sangha member helped us reduce our carbon footprint, because he knows a lot about energy audits, solar panels, and electric cars. Another member, a former banker, is on the board of Citizen's Climate Lobby and regularly lobbies in Washington for a carbon tax. I'm a member of 350.org, presently working to persuade the trustees of my alma mater to divest from fossil fuel stocks. Some members of the group also participated in a sit-in in front of a local bank that was financing an oil pipeline. Which of these actions is an appropriate response to the eco-crisis?

I would say all of them—and many more, including some perhaps unknown now but which will become important in the years to come. And which of them is "Buddhist," in the sense of being compatible with Buddhist teachings and practice? Again, I would say all of them—and many more. (See appendix 3, "Getting Real about Climate Change: Simple and Practical Steps.") In particular, I suspect that nonviolent civil disobedience will sooner or later become important, perhaps necessary—and that too is consistent with Buddhist teaching and practice.

That does not mean "anything goes" from a Buddhist perspective. Our ends, no matter how noble, do not justify any means, because Buddhism challenges the distinction between them. Its main contributions to our social and ecological engagement are the guidelines that the Theravada and Mahayana traditions offer. Although those principles have usually been understood in personal terms, as applicable to individual practice and awakening, the wisdom they embody is readily applied to the more collective types of engaged practice and social transformation that are needed today. Within Theravada, the five precepts (and Thich Nhat Hanh's engaged version of them) and the four "spiritual abodes" (brahmaviharas) are most relevant. The Mahayana tradition highlights the bodhisattva path, including the six perfections, and—perhaps the most important of all—the principle of acting without attachment to the results.

THE PRECEPTS

The traditional five precepts or "training rules" of the Pali Canon are to abstain from killing living beings (sometimes understood as not *harming* living beings), taking what is not given, sexual misconduct, improper speech, and intoxicating substances that dull the mind (such as alcohol or recreational drugs). It's important to understand that these are not "thou shalt not" commandments. Rather, they are vows that we take not to the Buddha or anyone else but to ourselves, with the conviction that *not* to live according to these principles is harmful to ourselves as well as to others, including the biosphere. Thich Nhat Hanh calls them "mindfulness trainings," replacing the usual "I undertake the precept to abstain from killing living beings," and so on, with "I undertake the course of training to abstain . . ." The emphasis on training avoids perfectionism by allowing for inevitable shortcomings. I vow to keep doing the best I can; when I break a precept, I don't indulge in self-recrimination but dust myself off and try again. As usual in Buddhism, sincere motivation is the most important thing.

Today it is difficult to overlook the social and ecological implications of these precepts. *Not to kill living beings* is broader than the injunction in the Mosaic Decalogue against murdering another human being, because members of other species are included. Traditionally this meant not being a soldier, butcher, or fisherman, for instance, but in this time of mass species extinction it implies reducing our participation in processes that contribute to harming other living beings. I say "reducing" because in such a complicated world economy it is virtually impossible to avoid some involvement. Palm oil, for example, is found in many of the products most of us use daily, and most of it comes from huge monocultural plantations planted after clear-cutting indigenous tropical forests, which destroys verdant ecosystems of plant and animal life. Although we can replace some of those products with healthier substitutes, the quest to become completely pure—free from any participation in an exploitative economic system—is never-ending and ultimately disempowering. There are more important things to focus on, such as challenging the institutions most responsible for promoting such clear-cutting.

A simpler and more direct response to the first precept is to reduce our consumption of animal products. According to the Pali Canon the Buddha was not vegetarian: monastics were mendicant, dependent on the food they were offered, so he forbade eating meat only if they knew or suspected that it had been slaughtered especially for them. Today massive factory farming of beef, pork, chicken, and increasingly seafood, too, not only involves incalculable suffering for the animals themselves but has major ecological implications. Mountains of excrement pollute water supplies, and ruminants release significant amounts of methane. Many millions of acres are necessary to produce all the animal fodder needed, an inefficient process that eventually provides us with sources of protein that are often unhealthy for various reasons. Whether or not one becomes completely vegetarian, it is important to reduce one's "food footprint."

Not taking what is not given is broader than our usual understanding of "not stealing." Today it is no longer acceptable to believe that the earth exists solely for the benefit of one species. We "own" it only in the sense that we have the power to exploit it. Our entire economic system is based upon taking what has not been given to us, because corporate globalization commodifies the whole earth and all its creatures into "natural resources" for the benefit of our species, especially a small global elite of our species. The ecological crisis is pushing us to realize that the earth does not belong to us; we belong to the earth.

No sexual misconduct is sometimes defined as "avoiding sex that causes pain or harm to others," and today we can see that this not only includes everyday sexual abuse (such as the #MeToo movement has exposed) but also has important collective dimensions, most obviously the burgeoning international sex trade, which exploits vulnerable women and children. That all of us have the same "empty" buddha-nature implies opposition to all forms of gender-based discrimination, especially patriarchal social structures that keep women in subservient positions. Ironically, this is also a serious problem for Buddhist institutions. Every Asian Buddhist culture is patriarchal, and in most of them women are not allowed to receive the full monastic ordination that men routinely do—despite support from the Buddha himself, according to the Pali Canon.

No improper speech includes abstaining from harsh language and gossip, but the biggest problem is lying, of course. Today, thanks to the internet, deception in the form of "fake news" has important political implications. Yet institutionalized deceit is not new insofar as increasingly concentrated corporate media have been using their enormous influence not to inform and educate but to manipulate for the sake of their true purpose, profits from advertising—including the marketing of political candidates. In addition to that, our attention is continually diverted by infotainment and the spectacles provided by sports and celebrity scandals. The functions of our national and international nervous systems—the media—are for sale to the highest bidder.

No harmful intoxicants traditionally focuses on alcohol, although obviously applicable to many other legal and illegal drugs. Today, however, what intoxicant clouds our minds more than the "never-enough" consumerism manipulated by a growth-obsessed economic system that needs to keep manufacturing markets for the goods it keeps exploiting the earth to produce? Thich Nhat Hanh understands this precept as "no abuse of delusion-producing substances," which can include television, social media, and cellphones, among other technological devices. As well as their obvious benefits, the addictive products of silicon chip miniaturization provide more opportunities to distract ourselves anytime and anyplace. If it is painful to stop and look at what we are doing to the earth and its other inhabitants—well, that is no longer a problem, because thanks to the wonders of modern technology we can evade such moments. Anytime we become bored, there's always a song or podcast to listen to.

In place of these five traditional precepts, Thich Nhat Hanh's book *Interbeing* offers fourteen precepts specifically intended for engaged Buddhism. These emphasize:

- Not being bound to any doctrines, even Buddhist ones, which includes openness to the viewpoints of others and not forcing others to accept your own views
- Not closing your eyes to the suffering in the world, but finding ways to be with those who are suffering
- Not pursuing fame, wealth, or sensual pleasure, but sharing resources with others who need them
- Letting go of anger and hatred when they arise
- Practicing mindful breathing to avoid dispersion and to return to what is happening in the present moment
- Avoiding words that are untruthful or cause discord
- Taking a clear stand against oppression and injustice, without engaging in party politics or partisan struggles
- Neither killing nor letting others kill; avoiding any vocation that involves harming humans or the natural world
- Respecting the property of others, while preventing others from profiting from the suffering of humans or other species

· Treating one's body and its vital energies with respect, which includes avoiding sexual expression without love and commitment

Thich Nhat Hanh's "engaged precepts," like the original five, basically tell us "don't do this!" All of them focus on what might be called *karmic traps* to be avoided, which enables us to engage with social and ecological issues more wholeheartedly and effectively. Buddhist teachings emphasize that we begin with our own transformation, to avoid projecting our own ego problems onto the world. I suggested above that following the "social precept" of *not taking what is not given* involves challenging an economic system that commodifies the earth's ecosystems into resources. But it also implies, first of all, challenging the individualized version in our own minds and lives—that is, learning to tread lightly on the earth and its other living beings. Voluntary simplicity, choosing to reduce our consumption, will not by itself be enough to reform the economic order, yet personally simplifying our lives in this way is also socially powerful because of the time and energy it liberates, and also because the example of an alternative lifestyle can be influential—especially if that lifestyle can be seen to reduce rather than aggravate one's dukkha.

In a similar fashion, we initially follow the social precept of *avoiding harmful intoxicants* by not allowing our own nervous systems to remain addicted to the channels of communication that maintain the collective trance of consumerism—today an important component of accepted "social reality." Instead, we accept responsibility for liberating our own attention and clarifying our own awareness, which usually requires some sort of meditation practice. Once grounded in that, we can work together more effectively to challenge the intoxicants purveyed by the media.

None of these precepts is uniquely Buddhist, of course. Many people who know little or nothing about Buddhism strive to live according to most or all of them. Mahatma Gandhi and Martin Luther King Jr. are obvious and inspirational examples. This suggests that the basic issue here is not principles that are distinctively Buddhist but a way of living that many other spiritual teachings also promote. Whether or not one identifies as Buddhist, attempting to embody these precepts encourages a similar transformation: one becomes less self-preoccupied and more engaged, as the sense of separation between one's own well-being and that of the world diminishes.

THE DIVINE ABODES

In addition to the five precepts that all Buddhists are encouraged to follow, the Buddha recommended the four brahmaviharas or "divine abodes," also known as the four sublime states: *metta* is usually translated as loving-kindness, *karuna* is compassion for the suffering of others, *mudita* is empathetic joy that shares in the happiness of others, and *upekkha* is imperturbable equanimity. They are divine abodes because, in the words of Joanna Macy, they "take you to the heart of reality. Then, for all intents and purposes, you are in heaven. You practice that loving-kindness; you look at everyone with those eyes of compassion and joy and equanimity, and there's nowhere else to go. You're home."

While the precepts are negative actions to avoid, the divine abodes are positive character traits to be developed. Once again, although the traditional focus is on individual transformation, they also have major consequences for social and ecological engagement. Taken together, all of these "dos" and "don'ts" provide a stable and powerful foundation for the kinds of spiritual activism needed today.

The Pali term *metta* derives from Sanskrit roots that originally meant friendly, affectionate, benevolent, with goodwill. In place of the common translation "loving-kindness," I prefer something like "basic friendliness" or "goodwill," which better describes the predisposition or baseline attitude with which one encounters people. This already has important implications for activism. Rather than approaching those who resist us (good people) as enemies (bad people) to be defeated, we enter into situations open to possibilities that are not foreclosed by such dualistic labeling.

Karuna (compassion) is one of the most important virtues in all Buddhist traditions, comparable only to *prajna*, the "higher wisdom" that is enlightenment. *Com-passion*—literally, "suffering with" (as in the "passion" of Christ)—is the essential trait to be developed in our practice and expressed in our lives. We are not indifferent to what others are feeling because we do not feel separate from them. Because, again, dukkha has traditionally been understood in individual terms—as a consequence of one's own karma and mental condition— the emphasis has usually been on personal assistance. The challenge for Buddhism today is connecting compassion with the structural causes of social and ecological dukkha.

Mudita is the happiness we feel when sharing in the well-being of others. Instead of the "suffering with" of compassion, one "enjoys with," like a mother delighting in the joy of her child. This trait complements *karuna*, which can otherwise overwhelm our ability to empathize. The vast amount of suffering in the world does not mean we should not be cheerful. In fact, if our relationship with the world is not also a source of happiness, our ability to address that suffering will itself suffer. Among other things, spending time in the natural world— communing with its other inhabitants, appreciating its serenity and beauty—can motivate and empower us to work for its well-being.

Upekkha, equanimity or "even-mindedness," literally means "to look over," to see without being captured by what is seen. More generally, it is the capacity not to be disturbed by what happens to us, as we experience the eight vicissitudes of life: gain and loss, praise and blame, pleasure and pain, fame and disrepute. According to Gil Fronsdal, equanimity "is the ground for wisdom and freedom and the protector of compassion and love. While some may think of equanimity as dry neutrality or cool aloofness, mature equanimity produces a radiance and warmth of being. The Buddha described a mind filled with equanimity as 'abundant, exalted, immeasurable, without hostility, and without ill-will.'" Nyanaponika Thera expands on its relationship with the other three brahmaviharas:

> Equanimity may be said to be the crown and culmination of
> the other three sublime states. The first three, if unconnected
> with equanimity and insight, may dwindle away due to the
> lack of a stabilizing factor. . . . It is the firm and balanced

character of a person that knits isolated virtues into an organic and harmonious whole, within which the single qualities exhibit their best manifestations and avoid the pitfalls of their respective weaknesses. And this is the very function of equanimity, the way it contributes to an ideal relationship between all four sublime states.

Without equanimity, it is difficult to avoid "burning out"—becoming so frustrated and angry that one gives up in despair. Notice, however, how Nyanaponika connects it with insight. Equanimity is not simply a character trait meditation develops; it becomes grounded in a realization about the nature of one's mind. In other words, it is characteristic of awakening. In Mahayana terms, it is an aspect of shunyata: insofar as my true nature is "empty" of any fixed form, ultimately there is no-thing to be disturbed. This has important implications for the bodhisattva path, as we shall see.

Before turning to that, however, there is another divine abode that I think deserves to be added to the traditional four brahmaviharas. Perhaps it is already implicit in the others, but if so, it merits more recognition, because "gratitude is not only the greatest of virtues, but the parent of all others" (Cicero).

Gratitude as an essential character trait brings us back to the spiral in Joanna Macy's "Work That Reconnects" (mentioned earlier), which begins with *coming from gratitude*, enabling us to *honor our pain for the world*, then *seeing with new eyes* and *going forth*. Gratitude, she says, "helps build a context of trust and psychological buoyancy that supports us to face difficult realities in the second phase." For Macy our gratitude for the earth and to the earth is not overwhelmed when compassion feels the earth's pain, but remains the foundation of the whole empowerment process.

According to the Dalai Lama, "The roots of all goodness lie in the appreciation of gratitude"—but in my case, it took a long time to appreciate the importance of that appreciation. Of course it's good to be grateful, so what's the point of emphasizing something so obvious? Eventually I realized something that hadn't been obvious, at least to me: gratitude is not just something you feel, or not, but a transformative *practice*. "The day I acquired the habit of consciously pronouncing the words 'thank you,' I felt I had gained possession of a magic wand capable of transforming everything" (Omraam Mikhael Aivanhov). Especially oneself.

In the Metta Sutta the Buddha recommends metta practice. In one popular version the practitioner radiates metta (the wish "may all beings be safe and happy") in all directions, starting with oneself—"may I be secure and happy"—and afterward extends the focus to include family and friends, followed by acquaintances, then people we don't like, and finally all beings in the universe. As Buddhist teachers like to point out, the one who benefits most from this practice is the person who does it, because it purifies our motivations and therefore our ways of relating to other people.

Something similar happens with gratitude practice. As Sarah Ban Breathnach expresses it, "Gratitude bestows reverence, allowing us to encounter everyday epiphanies, those transcendent moments of awe that change forever how we experience life (is it abundant or is it lacking?) and the world (is it friendly or is it hostile?)." There are two aspects to gratitude: appreciation of something and thankfulness directed to its source or cause. As we habitually reflect on all the things we can be grateful for, the two merge and become a facet of our character. According to James Baraz, who teaches Dharma courses on Awakening Joy, psychological studies show that depressives improve when they end each day by writing down ten things they're grateful for that happened that day.

In such exercises means and ends, the practice and its fruit, become the same thing.

This practice is all the more important because we live in a culture that does not encourage us to be grateful. In fact, we are encouraged not to be grateful: consumerism involves dissatisfaction, because if people are happy with what they've got, then they are less concerned about getting more. But (to say it again) why is more and more always better if it can never be enough? "If a fellow isn't thankful for what he's got, he isn't likely to be thankful for what he's going to get." (Frank A. Clark)

Our English word *gratitude* derives from the Latin *gratis*, meaning "for thanks," in the sense of "for nothing else in return, without recompense." We still use the term *gratis*, meaning something is "free of charge." Insofar as we are thankful, we participate in a gift economy rather than the exchange economy (where we pay for what we receive). Exchange emphasizes our separateness: transaction concluded, we go our own ways. Gratitude reinforces our connectedness: appreciation binds us together.

I cherish the way Meister Eckhart said it: "If the only prayer you ever say in your life is *thank you*, that will be enough."

THE BODHISATTVA PATH

Mahayana Buddhism developed a new conception of Buddhist practice: the bodhisattva path. In the Pali Canon the term *bodhisattva* refers to the earlier lives of Gautama before he became the Buddha. According to a common sectarian account, there was a conspicuous difference between his accomplishment and that of his followers, the *arahants* who awakened by following his teaching. An arahant (literally, "one who is worthy") has achieved the same nibbana as the Buddha, yet the Buddha was nonetheless special because he devoted himself single-mindedly and wholeheartedly to helping everyone awaken. This led to the development of a more altruistic paradigm of spiritual life that highlighted compassion, and which supposedly demonstrates the superiority of the Mahayana (literally, "Greater Vehicle") tradition over the Theravada, pejoratively called the Hinayana, "Lesser Vehicle."

It has been difficult for scholars to determine how much historical truth there is in this portrayal, but in any case it is important to distinguish the bodhisattva concept from self-serving doctrinal claims. The bodhisattva path is increasingly perceived by contemporary Buddhists in a nonsectarian fashion, as a inspirational archetype that embodies a new vision of human possibility—in particular, the alternative to rampant, self-preoccupied individualism, including any approach to Buddhist practice that is concerned only about one's own personal awakening. Understood in a more socially and ecologically engaged way, as ready to grapple with the collective and institutional causes of dukkha, the bodhisattva is precisely the spiritual paradigm we need today.

Doctrinally, a bodhisattva is a buddha-in-training following the example of Gautama Buddha—but with a twist. According to the Lankavatara Sutra, a bodhisattva "has taken the great vow: 'I shall not enter into final nirvana before all beings have been liberated.' He [or she] does not realize the highest liberation for himself, as he cannot abandon other beings to their fate. He has said: 'I must lead all beings to liberation. I will stay here till the end, even for the sake of one living soul.'"

This determination presupposes that "final nirvana" involves complete extinction without any rebirth, as supposedly happened to Gautama at his parinibbana. But there is another way to understand the ultimate goal: *apratishita-nirvana,* a "nonabiding nirvana" (or "nirvana of no abiding place") that neither abandons samsara nor seeks nirvana. Instead of feeling stuck in the one or trying to extinguish oneself in the other, the emphasis is on a nongrasping awareness that is free of all forms of attachment.

But isn't any vow to help all beings an attachment?

Not if one's compassion is a manifestation of something deeper than one's egoistic sense of self. Such bodhisattvas—or are they buddhas?—do not distinguish between samsara and nirvana, because spiritual equanimity does not mean indifference to what is happening in this world. In fact, such equanimity can be especially empowering, as we shall see.

As Joanna Macy writes:

> In every tradition, the spiritual journey seems to be presented in two ways. One is like a journey out of this messy, broken, imperfect world of suffering, into a sacred realm of eternal light. At the same time, within the same tradition, the spiritual journey is also experienced and expressed as going right

into the heart of the world—into this world of suffering and
brokenness and imperfection—to discover the sacred. . . .
This kind of liberation takes one not out of the world, but
right into it! It is a release into action.

This kind of liberation is also consistent with the understanding of
Buddhism presented earlier in this book: the path is not about transcending this world but realizing its true nature—that is, transcending our delusions about it, especially the delusion of a separate self
that is in the world but not of it.

According to Mahayana Buddhism, there are two very different
types of bodhisattvas. Celestial bodhisattvas are popularly believed to
be superhuman beings to whom one can appeal for help. They can
also be understood as archetypes that exemplify particular virtues. Of
the four main East Asian bodhisattvas, for example, Avalokiteshvara
(Guanyin in China, Kannon in Japan) is the foremost embodiment
of compassion, Manjushri personifies enlightened wisdom, Saman-
tabhadra represents creative activity, and Kshitigarbha symbolizes
fearlessness. We can relate to these figures as godlike beings available
to aid us when we call out to them, or as evoking our own human
capabilities.

That brings us to the other type of bodhisattva: you and me,
potentially. According to the classical formulation, we become
bodhisattvas—and the meaning of our lives is radically transformed—
when a particular aspiration arises spontaneously from somewhere
deep within us, from a place beyond self-interest because beyond our
usual sense of self.

The Buddhist term for this aspiration is bodhicitta—literally, "awakening mind" or "mind of enlightenment." That can mean a mind that
is awakened, or a mind that wants to awaken, or a mind that wants
to promote the awakening of everyone—or all three, which is best.
Bodhicitta is a wish or urge that arises naturally, motivated by deep
compassion, to awaken not just for one's own sake but for the benefit
of all sentient beings. According to the Dalai Lama,

> We should have this [compassion] from the depths of our
> heart, as if it were nailed there. Such compassion is not
> merely concerned with a few sentient beings such as friends
> and relatives, but extends up to the limits of the cosmos, in all
> directions and towards all beings throughout space.

The appearance of bodhicitta puts a bodhisattva on the path to full enlightenment, yet it seems to me that, if the urge that arises is truly spontaneous—if it springs up egolessly—then it is already a stage of enlightenment. Perhaps it is even the most important stage of enlightenment, because all the others tend to unfold naturally if that original motivation is acted upon and integrated into one's life.

According to traditional descriptions of the bodhisattva path, after bodhicitta arises one focuses on developing the six *paramitas* ("highest perfections"), attitudes that are cultivated and actions that are performed in a non-egocentric way.

The first paramita, *dana*—literally, "giving" or "generosity"—is sometimes said to contain all the other five. It is related to gratitude, being a way that gratitude is often expressed. Understood most broadly, it involves openhearted kindness to others gratis, with no expectation or desire for any return or reward. From the highest point of view, what I have is not mine because there is no me to possess it.

Sila, which can be translated as "virtue," "right conduct," or "discipline," incorporates the ethical precepts of early Buddhism discussed earlier. The emphasis is not on obedience or obligation but developing self-restraint and greater awareness of the effects of one's actions.

Kshanti, "patience," means an endurance that never takes offense or avoids an uncomfortable situation. The Dhammapada describes it as the "foremost austerity." In one early text, the Buddha exhorts his followers not to become hateful or speak angrily even if one's limbs are being sawed off by bandits.

Virya is variously translated as "energy" or "enthusiasm" or "sustained effort." It involves extreme perseverence or diligence: never giving up, in order to accomplish what is wholesome and to avoid what is unwholesome. Given the difficulties and frustrations of eco-activism, kshanti and virya stand out as especially important virtues to be developed.

Dhyana, "meditation," refers to the cultivation of mental concentration or contemplative practices, which are usually important for awakening.

Prajna—literally, "highest knowing"—is the wisdom that accompanies awakening. According to Mahayana it includes the realization that everything is shunya, "empty" of self-being, including oneself.

To be empty of my own self-being is to realize that I am not separate from you, in which case my well-being is not separate from yours and vice versa. As Shantideva says in his *Guide to the Bodhisattva's Way of Life*:

> Those desiring speedily to be
> A refuge for themselves and others,
> Should make the interchange of "I" and "other,"
> And thus embrace a sacred mystery.

> All the joy the world contains
> Has come through wishing happiness for others,
> All the misery the world contains
> Has come through wanting pleasure for oneself.

> May I be the doctor and the medicine
> And may I be the nurse
> For all sick beings in the world
> Until everyone is healed.

But what if it is the world itself—the earth—that is in misery? How do we nurse all sick beings back to health if the illness has become an epidemic? In that case we need to do more than treat the symptoms. We must identify and address the root causes.

The precepts, the divine abodes, and these six paramitas all involve the development of character traits that have traditionally been understood in individual terms, as furthering my own spiritual development and as helping me further the spiritual development of others—which further furthers my own spiritual development. For the bodhisattva, helping others on their spiritual path turns out to be an important part of one's own spiritual maturation.

Today, however, social justice issues and the ecological crisis are prompting reconsideration of the bodhisattva ideal. The traditional Buddhist focus on individual awakening and individual compassion was logical because consistent with the traditional focus on individual dukkha—on the suffering due to my own karma and the ways my own mind works. But what if one's suffering is not always due to what one has done or is doing now? What about the massive amounts of collective dukkha caused by institutions and other social structures? How might conventional conceptions of the bodhisattva path be adapted, to make Buddhist teachings more relevant to such challenges?

THE ECOSATTVA PATH

Buddhist teachings imply that an expanded, more socially engaged bodhisattva path will have some distinctive characteristics. For starters, Buddhist emphasis on interdependence ("we're all in this together") and delusion (rather than good versus evil) implies not only nonviolence (violence is usually self-defeating) but a politics motivated by love and compassion (more nondual) rather than anger (which dualizes between us and them). From a Buddhist perspective the basic problem is not rich and powerful "bad" people but institutionalized structures of collective greed, aggression, and delusion that need to be transformed. The Buddha's pragmatism and nondogmatism (his teachings are a raft to help us cross the river of samsara, not dogma to "carry on our backs") can help to cut through the ideological quarrels that have weakened so many progressive movements. And Mahayana emphasis on *upaya-kausalya* ("skill in means"; sometimes considered a seventh paramita)—the ability to adapt and respond successfully to new situations—foregrounds the importance of creative imagination, a necessary attribute if we are to co-construct a more sustainable way of living together on this planet.

Acknowledging the importance of social engagement is a big step for many Buddhists, who have usually been taught to focus on their own peace of mind. On the other side, those committed to social action tend to suffer from frustration, anger, depression, fatigue, and burnout. The engaged bodhisattva path provides what each needs, because it involves a double practice, inner and outer, in which the two sides not only balance but reinforce each other. While deeply engaged, bodhisattvas also remain committed to their personal practice, which normally includes some form of regular meditation. Meditation cultivates not only equanimity but the insight that supports it: awareness of that "empty" dimension where there is no better or worse, nothing to gain or lose. That perspective is especially important in especially difficult times, when one becomes overwhelmed by the magnitude of the task. The temptation, for Buddhist practitioners, is attachment to that dimension (often described as "clinging to emptiness") and therefore becoming indifferent to what is happening in the world. The problem, for activists, is on the other side: without the serenity cultivated by meditation they usually lack an imperturbable ground or stable basis for their lifework, which tends to weaken what they are able to contribute.

Combining the two practices enables intense engagement in goal-directed behavior with less exhaustion and burnout. Such activism also helps meditators avoid preoccupation with their own mental condition and progress toward enlightenment. Insofar as a sense of separate self is the basic problem, compassionate commitment to the well-being of others is an important part of the solution. Engagement with the world's problems is therefore not to be understood as a distraction from our personal spiritual practice but as essential to our own transformation. "People are always talking about practice, practice. What I want to know is, when is the performance?" (Robert Thurman). It turns out that performance—activism—is an essential part of the practice.

Cultivating insight and equanimity supports what is most distinctive and powerful about spiritual activism: the bodhisattva *acts
without attachment to the results of action.* Aphorism 28 of the Tibetan
lojong training offers a classic formulation: "Abandon any hope of fruition. Don't get caught up in how you will be in the future; stay in the
present moment."

I refer to "spiritual activism" rather than Buddhist activism because this principle is also an essential aspect of *karma yoga* in the
most important Hindu text, the Bhagavad Gita: "Your right is to the
work, never to the fruits. Be neither motivated by the fruits of action
nor inclined to give up action" (2:47).

Yet acting without attachment is easily misunderstood, suggest-
ing a casual attitude. "Yes, our local power company needs to convert from coal to renewables. We organized and protested for a while,
but there was a lot of resistance. It just didn't work. But that's okay,
because what's important are the intentions behind our actions, not
the results." That approach will never bring about the changes that
are necessary, because it misses the point about what nonattachment
really means.

To begin with, consider the difference between a marathon and
a 100-meter dash. When you run a 100-meter race, the only thing
that matters is sprinting to the goal as quickly as possible. You don't
have time to think about anything else. But you can't run a marathon
that way, because you'll soon exhaust yourself. Instead, you follow the
course without fixating on the goal line somewhere far ahead. If you
run in the right direction you will eventually get there, but in the process you need to focus on being here and now, just this step, just this
step . . . There is a Japanese term for it: *tada,* "just this!"

Dharma friends who do marathons tell me that this attitude can
lead to a "runner's high," when the running becomes effortless. This
is a taste of what Daoists call *wei wu wei*—literally, "the action of nonaction." When the (sense of) self temporarily merges or *becomes one*
with what the physical body is doing, one's usual sense of dualistic
effort disappears: the mind is no longer willing or pushing the body.

This type of nonaction does not mean doing nothing. The runner does not give up and sit by the side of the road in the belief that there's really no need to go anywhere. Instead, the running is a kind of "nonrunning" inasmuch as one is not rejecting the present moment in favor of a goal that will be achieved sometime in the future. Nonetheless, one is approaching the goal because one is doing what is needed right now: *just this!*

That is one aspect of nonattachment to the results of action, but there is more involved. Although a marathon is a long race, sooner or later one reaches the end and stops. What about a path with no end, with a task so difficult that it is difficult not to become discouraged?

In Japanese Zen temples, practitioners daily recite the four "bodhisattva vows." The first is to help all living beings awaken: "Sentient beings are numberless; I vow to liberate them all." If we really understand what this commitment involves, how can we avoid feeling overwhelmed? We are vowing to do something that cannot possibly be accomplished. Is that just crazy—or what?

That the vow cannot be fulfilled is not the problem but the very point. Since it can't be achieved, what the vow really calls for is reorienting the meaning of one's life, from our usual self-preoccupation to primary concern for the well-being of everyone. On a day-to-day level, what becomes important is not the unattainable goal but the direction of one's efforts—a direction that in this case orients us without providing any endpoint. What does that imply about how we respond to the eco-crisis? Someone who has already volunteered for a job that is literally impossible is not going to be intimidated by challenges because they sometimes appear hopeless!

No matter how momentous the task of working with others to try to save global civilization from destroying itself, that is nonetheless a small subset of what the bodhisattva has committed to doing. No matter what happens, we are not discouraged—well, not for long, at least. We may need a few mindful breaths first, but then we dust ourselves off and get on with it. That's because this vow goes beyond any attachment to any particular accomplishment—or defeat. When our efforts are successful, it's time to move on to the next thing. When they're not successful, we keep trying—indefinitely. Once we realize our nonduality with other people and with this magnificent planet that takes care of us all, we don't want to do anything else. It becomes our passion and our joy.

But that's not all. As the previous chapter discussed, there is the very real possibility that our efforts will not bring about the changes we seek. Privately, an increasing number of scientists are becoming pessimistic: we may be close to tipping points or have already passed them. It's difficult to anticipate what will happen, yet it doesn't look good. We just don't know.

"We just don't know." Hmmm . . . does that sound familiar? Isn't that something our contemplative practices cultivate: "don't know mind"? It is the first tenet of the Zen Peacemakers (the other two are bearing witness to the joys and suffering of the world and taking actions that arise from not-knowing and bearing witness). One of my Zen teachers, Robert Aitken, liked to say that our task is not to clear up the mystery but to make the mystery clear. The spiritual path isn't about coming to understand everything but opening up to experience a sacred and mysterious world where everything is changing whether or not we notice. Bodhisattvas access this mystery not by grasping it, in order to rest serenely in it, but in being taken by it. They manifest something greater than their egos.

This awesome mystery is not debilitating but empowering, because it liberates us from dogmatism and other fixed ideas about ourselves and the world. "The problem isn't what we don't know, but what we know that ain't so" (Josh Billings). We do the best we can in response to the best we know, although we never know for sure what's happening or what's possible. I grew up in a world defined by the Cold War between the West and the Soviet bloc, which everyone took for granted—until communism abruptly collapsed almost everywhere. Something similar occurred with South African apartheid soon thereafter.

Afterward, we can always find a chain of causes that reveal those events were inevitable—but that's in retrospect. If we don't even know what is happening now, how do we know what is possible, until we try?

This points to the deepest meaning of nonattachment to results. Our task is to do the very best we can, not knowing what the consequences will be—not knowing if our efforts will make any difference whatsoever. Have we already passed ecological tipping points and civilization as we know it is doomed? We don't know—and that's okay. Of course we hope our efforts will bear fruit, yet ultimately they are our gift to the earth, gratis.

We don't know if what we do is important, but we do know that it's important for us to do it. "Do not be daunted by the enormity of the world's grief. Act justly, now. Love mercy, now. Walk humbly, now. It is not your responsibility to finish the work [of *Tikkun olam*, healing the world], but you are not free to desist from it either." Rabbi Tarfon's famous saying is in the Jewish Mishnah, and the fact that it is found in yet another religious text is no coincidence. To act without attachment to results is very difficult for most of us, perhaps impossible, unless one has some spiritual foundation. Those committed to activism need the patience, perseverance, serenity, and insight that the bodhisattva path cultivates, along with the other divine abodes, including basic friendliness and joy in the well-being of others. And, I would add, all of that grounded in gratitude for our time together as one of the species created by this wondrous planet.

Of course, to be so unattached to the results of our efforts is to set the bar unrealistically high. Perhaps no one is able to embody the bodhisattva's double practice fully, any more than anyone's practice of the bodhisattva's six perfections will ever be perfect. And that's okay too. Our job is not to be perfect, but to do the best we can.

In conclusion, I wonder if the bodhisattva path may be the single most important contribution of Buddhism to our present situation. Is the earth itself today calling upon all of us to become bodhisattvas/ecosattvas?

Afterword

A Prodigal Species?

PERHAPS THE BEST-KNOWN PARABLE of Jesus is the story of the prodigal son. When we remember it, our minds usually turn to the penitent youth (us) and the forgiving father (God) who welcomes him home. But that's at the end of the story. The errant son is "prodigal" because of the way he squandered his inheritance: *prodigal*, after all, means "extravagant, wasteful, spendthrift, imprudent."

Can a species be prodigal? The similarity is hard to miss. According to Global Forest Watch, in just two years—2015 and 2016—the world lost enough trees to cover almost 500,000 square kilometers, nearly equal to the size of Spain. In addition to the pollution and land degradation mentioned in chapter 1, other natural resources are being exhausted, according to a 2016 report from the International Resource Panel of the UN's Environmental Program. The IRP co-chair Alicia Bárcena Ibarra emphasized that "the prevailing patterns of production and consumption are unsustainable." This "alarming rate . . . is already having a severe impact on human health and people's quality of life." Nonetheless, the top priority of those who control our economic and political institutions (which are really the two faces of one system) remains incessant economic growth.

The prodigal son left home to make his own way in the world, but he did not know how to manage his inheritance—what his father

bestowed on him. Isn't the same true of our inheritance, what the
earth has bestowed on us? The issue in both cases is not only lack
of worldly wisdom but a delusive sense of separation: leaving home,
literally or psychologically. The youth did not realize how fortunate
he had been until he experienced the consequences of his misspent
escapades far away; fortunately for him, also, it was not too late to
realize his mistake and make amends. We can assume that after returning he was more appreciative of family and home. We may hope
that he became a wise steward of the land, working for the well-being
of the whole.

We do not know if our collective story will have such a happy
ending.

Our species' sense of separation can be understood in various ways.
Mythologically it can be traced back to Adam and Eve. According to
the biblical account, they were expelled from the Garden of Eden for
disobeying God—the Old Testament deity being more punitive than
the prodigal son's father. From a Buddhist perspective, however, what
is most interesting about that account is that eating the forbidden fruit
opened their eyes, just as the serpent predicted. Realizing they were
naked—becoming self-conscious—Adam and Eve sewed fig leaves together to cover themselves and hide from God. Were they banished
from the Garden, then, or did they eject themselves, by coming to
feel separate from it? Did they really go somewhere else, or did they
simply experience where they were in a different way?

Their myth can be taken as a story about the transition from
hunting-gathering to agriculture—the origin of civilization as we
know it. God condemns them to painful toil tilling crops on ground
that more readily produces thorns and thistles. A curse indeed:
hunting-gathering peoples usually work less and enjoy a healthier
diet than do agriculturalists. Agriculture involved more labor, but it
created a surplus and the exploitive class hierarchies that appropriate it. It also signified a radical transformation in our relationship
with the earth, comparable in some ways to the difference between
a gift economy and an exchange economy. There is a sense in which
hunting-gathering societies belong to the earth, whereas the earth

belongs to sedentary civilizations, for whom land becomes property.

The Genesis account of creation provides the origin story for all the Abrahamic religions. In the first chapter of the Bible a radically transcendent God creates the heavens and the earth and all the plants and animals thereon, to be ruled by humans. The earth can be considered sacred insofar as God made it, but it and its creatures are nonetheless other than God and are also quite different from our species, which alone is "made in the image of God." Later we are promised eternity in a much better place, if we behave ourselves during our brief sojourn here. Already there is the ontological dualism that Loyal Rue identified as encouraging indifference to social and ecological problems. This world is devalued into a backdrop for the more important drama of human destiny. Some versions of Buddhism offer a similar story, by understanding nibbana as a transcendent escape from samsara, this world of suffering, craving, and delusion. In both cases alienation from the earth—not only our home but our mother—encourages us to distinguish its well-being from our own.

So what happens when our belief in such superior refuges evaporates? One would expect a revaluation of the secular world that remains, but when one half of the ontological dualism fades away, the other half does not automatically take up the slack. As we've seen, our postmodern mechanistic world remains haunted by the disappearance of God, the source of its meaning and value, a loss that has left us stranded in a desacralized universe, still alienated from our mother-home.

The basic problem with the modern worldview, I suspect, is that it provides no solution to our greatest fear, death. The point of ontological dualism—why it is so attractive—is that it offers the possibility of postmortem salvation. A secular universe that operates according to impersonal physical laws is unconcerned about us and our fate. In such a world, death is not the opening to another reality, just the end of this one. Unfortunately, our inability to accept mortality is also our inability to live fully here and now.

If so, we see again that the ecological crisis is not only a political or an economic or a technological issue but also a spiritual one, insofar as our relationship to death is a spiritual issue. On the individual level, the kind of transformation that is called for has been essential to Buddhism from the beginning. The Buddha left home because he encountered an old man, an ill man, and then a corpse. On the collective level, it is becoming ever more apparent that the mounting social and ecological challenges we face today require nothing less than a further development in human cultural evolution.

Throughout most of our history survival has naturally been the foremost concern, which meant that greed, aggression, and ego-delusion had an evolutionary function: those traits were selected for because they helped to get one's genes into the next generation. In a globalized postmodern world, with increasingly threatened ecosystems, those motivations have become counterproductive, yet we are still obsessed with economic growth/profit, militarism, and tribalism in various forms. It's comparable to our new problem with food. Until recently the threat that constantly loomed for most people was malnutrition if not starvation, but in developed countries the bigger issue now is obesity. Collectively as well as individually, different and more nondual motivations are called for, which require deconditioning and reconditioning ourselves.

That brings us to another prodigal son story, found in the most influential East Asian Buddhist scripture, the Lotus Sutra.

The Lotus Sutra version of the parable is more complex. In it, father and son are separated. The son wanders here and there and eventually becomes impoverished. His father, meanwhile, moves to another city where he becomes wealthy and respected. The son's wanderings eventually bring him to his father's estate. The father recognizes his son and sends servants to bring him in, but the son does not recognize his now-eminent father and runs away, frightened. Understanding his son's shame and fear, the father sends his servants, now disguised as menial workers, to offer him a job on the estate shoveling dung. When the son has become comfortable with this work, the father instructs his servants to gradually give him more responsibilities, until, years later, the son is managing the whole estate. Finally, when the father is about to die, he calls his friends and acquaintances together to reveal to them, and to his son, that this is really his son, to whom he leaves all his possessions. The sutra explains that the wealthy father is actually the Buddha, and we are his children, who will inherit his inexhaustible treasure.

The point of this story is that all of us have buddha-nature and are destined to become buddhas. The biblical parable is about good and evil: sin, repentance, and absolution. The father welcomes his son joyfully, all is forgiven and reconciliation is immediate. The Lotus Sutra version is about delusion and awakening: the son does not know who he really is and must transform in order to realize his true nature and manifest that exalted destiny.

Is this Buddhist version a better parable for our prodigal species? It's not enough for us to return home penitently—in our case, to realize that the earth is much more than a place where we happen to reside, that it is our mother, and that we have never severed the umbilical cord. Our strained relationship with the biosphere cannot be rectified as easily as that between the repentant son and his all-forgiving father. There is some serious work to do, in order to heal what has been damaged and thereby our relationship with it. Will that also heal us?

To become the species that the earth needs—creatures who are not only self-conscious but conscious that we are how the earth becomes self-conscious—we need to embrace the new bodhisattva path, which unites individual and social transformation. That involves contemplative practices deconstructing and reconstructing one's sense of self, in service of social and ecological engagement. Doing the best we can is our gift to the earth—in fact, since our species is one of its many ways of manifesting, it is really the earth's gift to itself.

The Lotus Sutra speaks of bodhisattvas springing forth from the earth, to preach the Dharma. It's time for ecosattvas to rise up from the earth and manifest the Dharma that defends and heals her.

Appendix 1:
The Time to Act
Is Now

A Buddhist Declaration on Climate Change

The declaration that follows was first published on the website ecobuddhism.org in 2009. It was composed as a pan-Buddhist statement by the Zen teacher Dr. David Tetsu'un Loy and the senior Theravadan teacher Ven. Bhikkhu Bodhi, with scientific input from Dr. John Stanley. The Dalai Lama was the first to sign this declaration.

TODAY WE LIVE in a time of great crisis, confronted by the gravest challenge that humanity has ever faced: the ecological consequences of our own collective karma. The scientific consensus is overwhelming: human activity is triggering environmental breakdown on a planetary scale. Global warming, in particular, is happening much faster than previously predicted, most obviously at the North Pole. For hundreds of thousands of years, the Arctic Ocean has been covered by an area of sea ice as large as Australia—but now this is melting rapidly. In 2007 the Intergovernmental Panel on Climate Change (IPCC) forecast that the Arctic might be free of summer sea ice by 2100. It is now apparent that this could occur within a decade or two. Greenland's vast ice sheet is also melting more quickly than expected. The rise in sea level this century will be at least one meter—enough to flood many coastal cities and vital rice-growing areas such as the Mekong Delta in Vietnam.

Glaciers all over the world are receding quickly. If current economic policies continue, the glaciers of the Tibetan Plateau, source of the great rivers that provide water for billions of people in Asia, are likely to disappear by midcentury. Severe drought and crop failures are already affecting Australia and northern China. Major reports from the IPCC, United Nations, European Union, and International Union for Conservation of Nature agree that, without a collective change of direction, dwindling supplies of water, food, and other resources could create famine conditions, resource battles, and mass migration by midcentury, perhaps by 2030, according to the United Kingdom's chief scientific advisor. Global warming plays a major role in other ecological crises, including the loss of many plant and animal species that share this earth with us. Oceanographers report that half the carbon released by burning fossil fuels has been absorbed by the oceans, increasing their acidity by about 30 percent. Acidification is disrupting calcification of shells and coral reefs, as well as threatening plankton growth, the source of the food chain for most life in the sea.

Eminent biologists and UN reports concur that "business as usual" will drive half of all species on earth to extinction within this century. Collectively, we are violating the first precept—"do not harm living beings"—on the largest possible scale. And we cannot foresee the biological consequences for human life when so many species that invisibly contribute to our own well-being vanish from the planet.

Many scientists have concluded that the survival of human civilization is at stake. We have reached a critical juncture in our biological and social evolution. There has never been a more important time in history to bring the resources of Buddhism to bear on behalf of all living beings. The four noble truths provide a framework for diagnosing our current situation and formulating appropriate guidelines— because the threats and disasters we face ultimately stem from the human mind, and therefore require profound changes within our minds. If personal suffering stems from craving and ignorance—from the three poisons of greed, ill will, and delusion—the same applies to the suffering that afflicts us on a collective scale. Our ecological emergency is a larger version of the perennial human predicament. Both as individuals and as a species, we suffer from a sense of self that feels disconnected not only from other people but from the Earth itself. As Thich Nhat Hanh has said, "We are here to awaken from the illusion of our separateness." We need to wake up and realize that the Earth is our mother as well as our home—and in this case the umbilical cord binding us to her cannot be severed. When the Earth becomes sick, we become sick, because we are part of her.

Our present economic and technological relationships with the rest of the biosphere are unsustainable. To survive the rough transitions ahead, our lifestyles and expectations must change. This involves new habits as well as new values. The Buddhist teaching that the overall health of the individual and society depends upon inner well-being, and not merely upon economic indicators, helps us determine the personal and social changes we must make.

Individually, we must adopt behaviors that increase everyday ecological awareness and reduce our "carbon footprint." Those of us in the advanced economies need to retrofit and insulate our homes and workplaces for energy efficiency; lower thermostats in winter and raise them in summer; use high efficiency light bulbs and appliances; turn off unused electrical appliances; drive the most fuel-efficient cars possible; and reduce meat consumption in favor of a healthy, environmentally friendly plant-based diet.

These personal activities will not by themselves be sufficient to avert future calamity. We must also make institutional changes, both technological and economic. We must "de-carbonize" our energy systems as quickly as feasible by replacing fossil fuels with renewable energy sources that are limitless, benign, and harmonious with nature. We especially need to halt the construction of new coal plants, since coal is by far the most polluting and most dangerous source of atmospheric carbon. Wisely utilized, wind power, solar power, tidal power, and geothermal power can provide all the electricity that we require

without damaging the biosphere. Since up to a quarter of world carbon emissions result from deforestation, we must reverse the destruction of forests, especially the vital rainforest belt where most species
of plants and animals live.

It has recently become quite obvious that significant changes are
also needed in the way our economic system is structured. Global
warming is intimately related to the gargantuan quantities of energy
that our industries devour to provide the levels of consumption that
many of us have learned to expect. From a Buddhist perspective, a
sane and sustainable economy would be governed by the principle
of sufficiency: the key to happiness is contentment rather than an
ever-increasing abundance of goods. The compulsion to consume
more and more is an expression of craving, the very thing the Buddha
pinpointed as the root cause of suffering.

Instead of an economy that emphasizes profit and requires perpet-
ual growth to avoid collapse, we need to move together toward an
economy that provides a satisfactory standard of living for everyone
while allowing us to develop our full (including spiritual) potential in
harmony with the biosphere, which sustains and nurtures all beings,
including future generations. If political leaders are unable to recognize the urgency of our global crisis, or unwilling to put the long-term
good of humankind above the short-term benefit of fossil fuel corporations, we may need to challenge them with sustained campaigns of
citizen action.

Dr. James Hansen of NASA and other climatologists have recently
defined the precise targets needed to prevent global warming from
reaching catastrophic "tipping points." For human civilization to
be sustainable, the safe level of carbon dioxide in the atmosphere is
no more than 350 parts per million (ppm). This target has been en-
dorsed by the Dalai Lama, along with other Nobel laureates and distinguished scientists. Our current situation is particularly worrisome
in that the present level is already 387 ppm, and has been rising at 2
ppm per year. [In May 2018 it is 412.6 ppm.] We are challenged not

only to reduce carbon emissions, but also to remove large quantities of carbon gas already present in the atmosphere.

As signatories to this statement of Buddhist principles, we acknowledge the urgent challenge of climate change. We join with the Dalai Lama in endorsing the 350 ppm target. In accordance with Buddhist teachings, we accept our individual and collective responsibility to do whatever we can to meet this target, including (but not limited to) the personal and social responses outlined above.

We have a brief window of opportunity to take action, to preserve humanity from imminent disaster and to assist the survival of the many diverse and beautiful forms of life on Earth. Future generations, and the other species that share the biosphere with us, have no voice to ask for our compassion, wisdom, and leadership. We must listen to their silence. We must be their voice, too, and act on their behalf.

Appendix 2:
Sixteen Core Dharma Principles to Address Climate Change

From the One Earth Sangha

THE FOLLOWING DHARMA principles directly apply to the issue of climate disruption:

1. *Reverence for life*: From this point forward climate disruption is the overriding context for all life on earth, including humans. What we humans do will determine what life survives and thrives and in what form and locations.

2. *Happiness stems from helping others*: Our greatest personal happiness comes when we give of ourselves and help others. For example, many people instinctually help our neighbors after a natural disaster, which indicates that altruism and the desire to help others is built into our genes. We must grow and apply this to the marginalized among us that are at least initially hit hardest by climate disruption. This is the very opposite of the greed and self-centeredness that dominates today.

3. *We suffer when we cling*: The very nature of happiness is dependent on our capacity to give up our attachments and help others. This same principle must now be elevated and applied to public policies of all types.

4. *The ethical imperative*: All beings matter. We should act in ways that are beneficial for both self and others, acting out of a commitment to altruism and compassion for others.

5. *Interconnection and interdependence*: We must dissolve objectification of other people and nature and overcome the belief in a separate self that leads us to through a sense of kinship. Even as we let go of the delusion of an individual self that is separate from other people, we must let go of the delusion that humanity is separate from the rest of the biosphere. Our interdependence with the earth means that we cannot pursue our own well-being at the cost of its well-being. When the earth's ecosystems become sick, so do our bodies and our societies.

6. *Renunciation, simplicity*: To resolve climate disruption we must be willing to renounce attachments to things that contribute to the problem and live more simply.

7. *The relationship between the first and second noble truth and capacity to learn to work with difficult states*: We must understand the suffering we have created symbolized by climate disruption and how it came about and that we can learn not to identify with it and instead work through distressing states such as fear and despair.

8. *Opening to suffering as a vehicle for awakening*: The suffering caused by climate disruption provides an unprecedented opportunity for humans to learn from our individual and collective mistakes and manifest a great awakening. It is a special opportunity like never before. We can find ways to be happy—we can "tend and befriend" rather than fight (among ourselves), flee, or freeze. We can acknowledge that this is the way things are now, open to the suffering rather than becoming attached, and think and act in new ways.

9. *The interconnectedness of inner and outer, the individual and the collective (or institutional)*: Climate disruption provides an unprecedented opportunity to understand the roots of the problem—which relate to the ways our minds work and how those patterns become embedded in collective and collective/institutional prac-

tices and policies. This awareness can open the door to new ways of thinking and responding that will eventually produce different institutional practices and policies.

10. *Connection to diversity and justice issues*: The Dharma principles and narratives must also apply to issues of diversity and social inclusion and justice. The beliefs in separateness and so forth that have produced the climate crisis also lead to social inequity and exclusion. People of color and other marginalized groups must be included.

11. *Buddhism as a social change agent*: The principles of Buddhism help us engage with life, not remove ourselves from it. The Buddha was actively engaged with his social and cultural contexts, and for Buddhism to have relevance today it must help people understand how to engage in today's political and social contexts.

12. *Adhitthana or determination*: We are called to develop resolve, determination, and heroic effort now. We must have the courage to realize that we are being called to engage in this issue and that living the Dharma will see us through the hard times.

13. *This precious human birth is an opportunity*: We must always remember that it is a rare and precious thing to be born as a human and we have been given a rare opportunity to act as stewards because humans are not only the source of destruction—we are also the source of great goodness.

14. *Love is the greatest motivator*: Our deepest and most powerful action comes out of love: of this earth, of each other. The more people can connect with and feel love for the earth, the greater the likelihood that their hearts will be moved to help prevent harm. Children should therefore be a top priority. We need to help people realize what they love about life and what will be lost as climate disruption increases.

15. *The sangha—and other forms of social support—are essential*: The reality of climate disruption is a profound shock to many people, and the only way to minimize or prevent fight, flight, freeze responses is to be supported by and work with others so people

will not feel alone, can overcome despair, and develop solutions together. We need to go through this journey together, sharing our difficult reactions and positive experiences in groups and communities.

16. *The bodhisattva*: The figure of the bodhisattva, which is a unifying image of someone who is dedicated to cultivating the inner depths and to helping others, is an inspiring figure for our times.

(FROM ONEEARTHSANGHA.ORG/ARTICLES/16-PRINCIPLES)

Appendix 3:
Getting Real
about Climate Change

Simple and Practical Steps

CURRENT DISCOURSE ON climate change among "progressives" often pivots around two themes, depending on where they stand on the spectrum:

- Spiritual progressives (including many Buddhist teachers) say that to stop climate change we need a "spiritual awakening of humanity," "the enlightenment of all beings," the "emergence of a divine humanity."
- Political progressives say that we need to change the whole political economy, to replace capitalism with a new social and economic system.

Granted that both these goals are desirable, are they realistic solutions to the immediate climate crisis? This seems improbable:

- Humanity is unlikely to undergo a dramatic spiritual rebirth in the short time left to us, while ever more nations seek to embark on the path of economic development by burning fossil fuels.

- Transformations in our social and economic system are likely to occur gradually and to require a long stretch of time for their impact to be felt.

However, we face a situation of utmost urgency:

- Urgent because of what is at stake: mass extinctions; famines, droughts floods, and epidemics; traumatic ethnic, religious, and cross-border strife; the loss of human civilization.
- Urgent because the window of opportunity is closing: we have at best only twenty or thirty years left to reduce carbon emissions by 80 percent; even better, to be on the safe side, we should aim at 100 percent reduction by 2040. And we are moving in that direction far too slowly, if at all.

To emerge intact, we've got to get real. Spiritual people and progressives in particular have got to be practical and realistic. So what can we do that is simple, practical, and realistic—though by no means easy?

I. TO ABSTAIN FROM ALL EVIL (APPLICATION OF THE STICK)

1. *Impose a moratorium* on fossil fuel extraction: no more auctioning of public lands, offshore drilling, mountaintop mining; keep it in the ground, in the hills, and in the seas.
2. *Rescind subsidies* to fossil fuel corporations.
3. *Impose a carbon tax* to ensure environmental costs are built into the market price of carbon; distribute the revenue to the public.
4. *Reject trade agreements* that allow corporations to prevail over sovereign governments.
5. *Reject mega pipelines*: though Keystone XL is gone, other pipelines are being built within the country.
6. *Prohibit oil trains* ("train bombs"), a danger to communities along the routes.
7. *Shift away from a model of industrial agriculture* responsible for 30–32 percent of global carbon emissions.

II. To cultivate the good (offering carrots)

1. *Provide subsidies* and low-interest loans *to clean, renewable energy* projects.

2. Finance *refurbishing of old buildings* to make them energy-efficient.

3. Promote mass production of *electric and hybrid cars.*

4. Develop *more and better public transit* to replace private cars.

5. Promote *agro-ecological models* to replace industrial agriculture.

6. Shift to more *climate-friendly diets* (plant-based over meats).

III. To purify one's own mind

1. Promote *contentment and simplicity,* the basis for a steady-state economy based on the principle of sufficiency, dedicated to qualitative growth rather than endless production and consumption.

2. Utilize *wisdom,* to understand the long-range and long-term consequences of our actions, rooted in the subtle interconnections of diverse chains of causality.

3. Arouse a heart of *compassion,* extend loving concern to all people everywhere, based on deep inner identification and affirmation of human dignity.

4. Advocate for *justice,* to establish social, economic, and political institutions and laws, enabling everyone to unfold their potentials and realize their aspirations.

IV. To benefit all sentient beings. How?

1. *Vote:* Though the political system is badly flawed, elections can make a difference. Vote only for candidates who admit human-caused climate change and are willing to act against it.

2. *Write and sign:* Write letters to your representatives, senators, and others. Call their offices and sign petitions and appeals to be sent to them. Local action may be most effective.

3. *Support "mom & pop" businesses:* Move our money, protect our planet: divest from fossil fuel corporations and related firms.

4. *Get moving*: Participate in marches and demonstrations to convey a message to those in power. Get moving in another way too; join a movement to protect the climate: BCAN, 350.org, Climate Mobilization, Greenpeace, the Next System Project.

5. *Take direct action*: Work to block climate-destroying projects, such as oil rigs, pipelines, and fracking sites, for instance. Beware of the risks of long prison terms, large fines.

(PREPARED BY VEN. BHIKKHU BODHI, 2016)

Appendix 4:
The Ecosattva Vows

I VOW TO MYSELF and to each of you:

To commit myself daily to the healing of our world
And the welfare of all beings.

To live on earth more lightly and less violently
in the food, products, and energy I consume.

To draw strength and guidance from the living Earth,
the ancestors, the future generations,
and my brothers and sisters of all species.

To support others in our work for the world
and to ask for help when I need it.

To pursue a daily practice
that clarifies my mind, strengthens my heart,
and supports me in observing these vows.

—from *Active Hope: How to Face the Mess We're in
without Going Crazy,* by Joanna Macy and Chris Johnstone

At the Rocky Mountain Ecodharma Retreat Center

Appendix 5:
The Rocky Mountain
Ecodharma Retreat Center

A Home for Meditation in Nature

INSPIRED BY THE ECODHARMA CENTRE in Spain, but not affiliated with it, the Rocky Mountain Ecodharma Retreat Center is a new dharma center that opened in the summer of 2017. It is half an hour by car from north Boulder and about ninety minutes from Denver International Airport. The center includes a lodge (which can accommodate up to thirty people), a covered pavilion, and a caretaker's cabin, on 180 acres of private river, meadows, and woodland adjacent to a national forest. Just a few miles from the Indian Peaks Wilderness and with breathtaking views of the Rocky Mountains, the land is set aside as a nature preserve and home to an abundance of wildlife including deer, elk, moose, bear, and beaver.

RMERC brings Buddhist teachings and practice back into the natural world where they originated, helping practitioners regain the connection and energy necessary to effectively address ecological and social challenges. The emphasis is on learning from nature and discovering ourselves in a wild environment. Activities include:

- Ecodharma retreats and workshops for activists, using the healing power of meditation in nature to ground and transform activism into a spiritual path of service to the community and the earth.

- Low-cost retreats that are offered in the spirit of generosity, with teachers receiving only expenses and donations (dana).
- Silent meditation retreats, in groups and also on supported solos. All spiritual practice traditions are welcome, and local sanghas are encouraged to use RMERC for weekends and day-longs as well as for longer retreats.
- Retreats and other activities for underserved communities including people of color, veterans, youth, and other groups who have historically borne (or will bear) the brunt of ecological and socioeconomic devastation and are often at the front of spiritually rooted activism.

Learn more at www.rockymountainretreatcenter.org.

For me in this dark time, Rocky Mountain Ecodharma Retreat Center will be a shining beacon I can trust. I see it offering what we most need: the inspired leadership of committed teachers, a wild mountain setting to awaken our own power and beauty, the ripening of a Sangha to grow a guiding vision for our people, and the strength to make it real.

—JOANNA MACY

Acknowledgments
and Credits

First of all, thanks yet again to Josh Bartok, Ben Gleason, and Lindsay D'Andrea—and the other fine folks at Wisdom Publications, for all their work bringing this project to fruition. I could write this book without worrying about the fruits of my labors because I knew that afterward it would be in their very capable hands.

There are many others to thank as well, beginning with Joanna Macy, Bhikkhu Bodhi, and Guhyapati, three of the great ecosattvas of our time. Joanna formulated the "Ecosattva Vows," and Bhikkhu Bodhi put together the "Simple and Practical Steps." Guhyapati is the founder of the Ecodharma Centre in Spain. The "Sixteen Core Dharma Principles" were compiled by the Dharma Teachers Climate Cooperative. More contributions by them (and others) are available at oneearthsangha.org, the website of One Earth Sangha, founded by Kristin Barker and Lou Leonard.

"The Time to Act Is Now: A Buddhist Declaration on Climate Change" first appeared on ecobuddhism.org. I am especially grateful to John Stanley and Diane Stanley, who created and maintained it. Along with Gyurje Dorme and myself, John also coedited *A Buddhist Response to the Climate Emergency*, a book ahead of its time. I also want to express my appreciation for the contributions of the other board members of the new Rocky Mountain Ecodharma Retreat Center:

especially the executive director, Johann Robbins, who has done most of the work, but also Kritee Kanko, Peter Williams, Russ Hullet, Anne Kapuscinski, and Jeanine Canty. Janine Ibbotson and Alice Robbins have also done a lot to get the center started.

Many others have contributed (sometimes without knowing it) to the gestation of this book and/or the development of ecodharma. In addition to the above, and all those who contributed to *A Buddhist Response to the Climate Emergency*, I offer a deep bow to Jon Aaron, Elias Amidon, David Bachrach, Rob Burbea, Lloyd Burton, Angels Canadell, David Chernikoff, Grant Couch, Ron Davis, Sherry Ellms, Gil Fronsdal, Belinda Griswold, Patrick Groneman, Joan Halifax, Dawn Haney, Fletcher Harper, Robert Ho, Jeff Hohensee, Vince Horn, Mushim Ikeda, Chris Ives, Ken Jones, Stephanie Kaza, Terry Kinsey, Robert Kolodny, Taigen Dan Leighton, Michael Lerner, Katie Loncke, Zenju Earthlyn Manuel, Willa Miller, Susan Murphy, Rod Owens, Anne Parker, Jordi Pigem, Ron Purser, Elizabeth Roberts, Alice Robison, Marcia Rose, Donald Rothberg, Santikaro, Alan Senauke, Henry Shukman, Mu Soeng, Emma Stone, Bonnie Sundance, Thanasanti, Thanissara, Daniel Thorson, Jesus Blas Vicens, Jon Watts, angel Kyodo williams, Jason Wirth, Janey Zietlow . . . with apologies to all those whose names I'm forgetting.

And last but certainly not least, thanks again to Linda Goodhew for sharing her life with me and taking care of me while this book was being written—and during other times too.

Index

About the Author

DAVID LOY began Zen practice in Hawaii in 1971 with Yamada Koun and Robert Aitken, and continued with Koun Roshi in Japan, where he lived for almost twenty years. He was authorized to teach in 1988 and leads retreats and workshops nationally and internationally at places such as Spirit Rock, Barre Center for Buddhist Studies, Omega Institute, Cambridge Insight Center, Terre d'Eveil in Paris, and Dharma Gate in Budapest. David is a professor of Buddhist and comparative philosophy, and recently received an honorary PhD from his alma mater, Carleton College, for his scholarly work on socially engaged Buddhism. (Later he returned this degree to protest the trustees' decision not to divest the college endowment from fossil fuel investments.)

David is a well-known writer whose books and articles have been translated into many languages. His recent works include *A New Buddhist Path* and the second edition of *Lack and Transcendence*. He has written many articles and blog posts on Buddhism, ecology, and activism. He is also vice president of the new Rocky Mountain Ecodharma Retreat Center. Many of David's writings, podcasts, and videos are available at www.davidloy.org.

What to Read Next
from Wisdom Publications

A New Buddhist Path
Enlightenment, Evolution, and Ethics in the Modern World
David R. Loy

"This gripping, important, and ultimately heartening book by David Loy is a wake-up call for Buddhists and everyone else on how to respond to the current multiple crises."—Lila Kate Wheeler, author of *When Mountains Walked*

Money, Sex, War, Karma
Notes for a Buddhist Revolution
David R. Loy

"A flashy title, but a serious and substantial book."—*Buddhadharma*